101 Lightbulb Moments

in Data Management

101
LIGHTBULB
MOMENTS
in
DATA MANAGEMENT
TALES FROM THE **DATA ROUNDTABLE**
Edited by Phil Simon

Contributors:

Jill Dyché

Jim Harris

Dylan Jones

David Loshin

Joyce Norris-Montanari

Rich Murnane

Phil Simon

Motion Publishing, LLC
Las Vegas. Nevada

101 Lightbulb Moments in Data Management
Tales from the **Data Roundtable**
Edited by Phil Simon
© 2011 DataFlux

Motion

www.motionpub.com
Published by Motion Publishing, LLC
Las Vegas, Nevada.
ISBN-13: 978-0-9829302-9-8
ISBN-10: 0-9829302-9-1
Library of Congress Control Number: 2011938249
FIRST PAPERBACK EDITION
Printed in the United States of America

Editor and Production Director: Sue Collier
Cover Designer: Jennifer King
Interior Designer: Juanita Dix
Proofreader: Karen A. Gill

Table of Contents

PART III: DATA GOVERNANCE

In God we trust; all others must bring data.

—W. Edwards Deming (1900–1993)

101 Lightbulb Moments in Data Management
Foreword

A "lightbulb moment" occurs at the point where inspiration meets action. Sometimes the inspiration is immediate and unexpected. Often, however, inspiration comes after spending a significant amount of time researching a problem and searching for a solution. There can be both failures and frustration before a breakthrough. But a lightbulb moment marks the point where things start falling into place and results start becoming visible.

Think about Thomas Edison. He enjoyed many lightbulb moments during his life, demonstrated by the 1,093 U.S. patents he holds for inventions that include a stock ticker, a mechanical vote recorder, a battery for an electric car, electrical power, recorded music, and motion pictures. For one of his first groundbreaking inventions, Edison took the knowledge from other inventors who had already produced electric lightbulbs and combined it with his own idea to use a carbon filament inside the bulb. The result was the first commercially viable incandescent light. It was a perfect example of inspiration combined with hard work and experimentation.

This book, *101 Lightbulb Moments in Data Management*, contains bright ideas that can help you overcome the short circuits in your data management projects and build on your inspirations. It provides new thoughts and approaches that you can apply to your organization as you transform your corporate data into a valuable asset.

The contributors to this book have truly "been there" and "done that" in the data management world. They are noted contributors to the Data Roundtable, a thought leadership site sponsored by DataFlux. I have had the opportunity to work with them over the years, both as colleagues and partners. They are the data contributors that companies turn to with the thorniest data management challenges. They understand the power of data and its importance in driving a business forward. Today, perhaps more than ever, companies need to harness that power. Properly managed data will help you make better decisions.

I hope you enjoy these lightbulb moments and that this book serves as the filament of your own bright ideas.

Part I:
Data Management

Organizations continue to struggle managing their data. For all sorts of reasons, effective data management seems to elude companies of every size. This is particularly difficult as organizations amass more—and more types of—data. The rise of unstructured data presents organizations with unique challenges, from both management and data mining perspectives. What good is data if you can't use it, access it, and ultimately make better decisions from it?

Fret not, as the contributors answer important questions like these and provide compelling insights in this section.

Idea 1: The Data Avalanche Is Coming. Are You Ready?
Dylan Jones

Can you hear it?

It's just a distant rumbling, but already there are visible signs of the impending deluge of data that is about to hit your organization.

- In the financial sector, market data is growing at a phenomenal rate.
- In telecoms, the impending distribution of SIM cards in appliances and the rush to develop new customer experience channels across the connected web will create a tsunami of data.
- In retail, the continuous expansion of web-enabled service delivery is creating greater volumes and complexity on a daily basis.

The list goes on.

The technology infrastructure will probably adapt and cope. New disruptions create new opportunities, and this in turn creates new advances. We're constantly hearing of game-changing innovations in processing, storage, ventilation, and transmission.

But how will this data avalanche affect your company?

- Master data will increase as we store further subject areas such as customers, products, services, and locations.
- Reference data is rapidly expanding into the cloud and becoming far more open source. Expect in-house volumes to rise as a result.
- Transaction data will no doubt increase, particularly where greater regulatory involvement necessitates access to longer transaction histories and more transparency.
- Analytical data held in data warehouses and staging areas such as data marts will have to rise to cope with the upstream growth.

The increase in data volumes will invariably lead to an increase in defective data if programs of data governance and data quality are ignored.

What is interesting is that many analysts are not predicting a linear rise in data volumes. Far from it.

Measurements from Six Sigma projects show us that as defects increase linearly, the actual impact on the workforce and service performs degrades in a nonlinear fashion. If we have a nonlinear rise in defects coupled with a nonlinear rise in service impact, what will this mean for customer-facing organizations? Many are already constant press and social media fodder for their poor customer experience.

This is not a problem that technology alone can resolve. For most companies it requires a seismic cultural shift in how every person in the organization perceives and manages data. Systems and information technology (IT) infrastructure can evolve endlessly, but you can't buy a culture of data quality. It takes time—sometimes many years—to create a vision, a sense of urgency, and an ability to adapt.

> It takes time—sometimes many years—to create a vision, a sense of urgency, and an ability to adapt.

Consider that by 2013, some analysts suggest that mobile commerce is set to double in the UK alone. In other countries, the figures are much higher.

So when you're considering rejection of that business case for data quality or data governance, consider the data landscape in five years' time.

Idea 2: The Decentralized Data Quality Movement
Joyce Norris-Montanari

Does it work well for a corporation if each department has its own data quality initiative? I call this the Data Quality Movement because each department knows it needs to pay attention to data quality, but the corporation hasn't decided how to manage the quality of the data across the organization. Departments end up handling data quality on their own as a result.

Centralized data quality would come from the enterprise data management group, but most of these groups are not thinking about master data or corporate data. Employees don't have time to manage a platform for data quality and data integration for the corporation. What that means is that most are not ready for a corporate initiative and are really not sure how to go about implementing one.

> Most are not ready for a corporate initiative and are really not sure how to go about implementing one.

Would it help if employees had the following?

- **Enterprise guidelines for departmental data management:** For example, how do employees use enterprise metadata about data, and how do they contribute information for consumption?
- **Enterprise software to manage the data quality and data integration:** This would require a single platform for all the metadata—a platform that could eliminate re-creation of the same data analysis metadata.
- **Personnel who really understand the concepts of data management for the enterprise:** This is the hard one. Personnel think they understand how to do this, but they've never really implemented data management for a large organization.

A roadmap is needed for how to bite off small chunks for implementation. This requires management buy-in and corporate participation. Furthermore, corporate participation requires education and adherence.

Idea 3: Master Data Consolidation
David Loshin

I have long advised clients that adopting a master data approach without having a master data strategy may lead to uncontrolled data consolidation without the benefit of the right kinds of controls to prevent confusion. Here is a good example: the offices for Knowledge Integrity are at one location, while we live at another location. Our company has a 401(k) plan with an investment company, and as president of the company, I am

a trustee for the 401(k) plan. Therefore, mail with my name on it associated with the plan is supposed to go
to our business address. However, as
an employee of my own company, I
also have a 401(k) account. The mail
associated with that account should
go to our home address.

> Adopting a master data
> approach without having
> a master data strategy
> may lead to uncontrolled
> data consolidation with-
> out the benefit of the
> right kinds of controls to
> prevent confusion.

However, I found that all the mail
that had my name on it was going to
the business address (both account and plan correspondence). I contacted
the company and explained that I expected my account records to be sent
to my home account. "No problem," the rep said, while changing the address for my correspondence to the home address. The next thing I knew,
the 401(k) plan correspondence also started coming to the home address.
So I called the 401(k) company back and requested that the business correspondence go to the business address. "No problem," the rep said while
changing the address for my correspondence to the business address. Of
course, now the mail is back to the way it was before—all letters come to
the business address.

Of course, I know what is going on here: the company's customer consolidation process does not allow for an individual to operate in more than
a single role when it comes to location/contact mechanism. Changing one
contact mechanism associated with the unique entity changes it for all roles
the entity plays. This is a failure in the company's modeling process since it
is unwilling to accommodate multiple roles for unique entities.

Idea 4: The Importance of Scope in Data Quality Efforts
Jill Dyché

When it comes to data quality, I fervently believe that it is destined for
widespread adoption. As a concept, data quality has been around for a while,
but until now it's only truly been appreciated by a group of aficionados. But

just like taco trucks, the HBO show *In Treatment,* video on demand, and Adam Lambert, data quality's best days are actually ahead of it.

Part of the reason data quality hasn't yet hit its stride is because it remains a difficult sell. Those of us in the business intelligence and data integration communities understand that accurate and meaningful data is a business issue. And well intentioned though they may be, IT people have gone about making the pitch the wrong way.

We—vendors, consultants, and practitioners in the IT community—blather on about data quality being a business issue and requiring a business case and a repeatable set of processes, but at the end of the day automation remains the center of most data quality discussions. As executives try to explain the return on investment (ROI) of name and address correction, deterministic matching, multisource data profiling, and the pros and cons of the cloud, they are thinking two things:

- "I'm bored."
- "I wonder how we would start something like this? Where would we begin?"

In fact, the topic of scope is a huge gaping hole in the data quality conversation. As we work with clients on setting up data governance, we often use the bad reputation of corporate data as its pretext. We always, always talk about the boundaries of the initial data quality effort. Unless you can circumscribe the scope of data quality, you can't quantify its value.

In our experience, there are five levels of data quality delivery that can quickly establish not only the scope of an initial data quality effort but the actual duties and resources involved in the initial project (see Figure 1 on page 6).

We're also more likely to be solving a real-life problem. Thus, we make the initial win much more impactful, thus securing stakeholder participation. Moreover, where we start our data quality effort is not necessarily where we'll finish, so we can ensure

> By specifying the initial scope of the data to be corrected, we're establishing the boundaries of the effort itself.

an incremental approach to setting up the program and its roles.

By specifying the initial scope of the data to be corrected, we're establishing the boundaries of the effort itself.

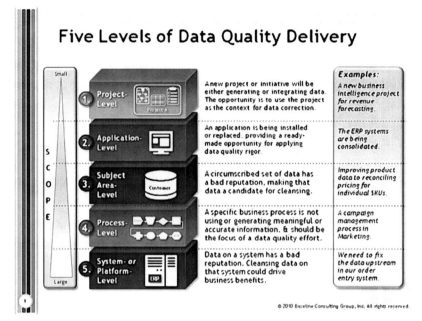

Figure 1: Five Levels of Data Quality Delivery

Business executives and users can consume a well-scoped problem, especially if it makes their jobs easy or propels progress. And if we solve it in a way that benefits the business—eliminating risk, ensuring economies of scale, and driving revenues—we might even get budget for a data quality tool!

Idea 5: The Seven-Year Glitch
Jim Harris

In 2003, I purchased a townhouse in Ankeny, a northern suburb of Des Moines, Iowa. I made a 20 percent down payment on my townhouse, which, in the United States, meant that I didn't need to purchase private mortgage insurance. I then secured a 7/23 adjustable-rate mortgage, which meant I'd have a fixed interest rate for the first seven years of a thirty-year mortgage that would thereafter adjust on an annual basis. I also purchased a homeowners insurance policy.

With the initial interest rate on my current loan due to expire at the end of this year, my current mortgage company began sending me letters of notification. One of the letters informed me that I had never secured the appropriate amount of insurance for my townhouse and, as it was my responsibility to protect the insurance company's financial best interests, if I did not remedy this situation, I was at risk of foreclosure. I ignored this letter because, as I previously explained, I had secured the appropriate amount of insurance.

A follow-up letter informed me that, out of the glowing kindness of the mortgage company's heart (and apparently with a passing consideration of the fact that I had never been late with a single mortgage payment in seven years), it would not foreclose on me and would not be evicting me from my townhouse. (How very nice of them, eh?)

Instead, the company would secure the appropriate amount of insurance for my townhouse through its insurance company—and send me the bill for $2,000 USD a month for the premiums. (My actual homeowners insurance cost only $200 USD a year.) Therefore, I decided to take all the letters from my current mortgage company and go see my insurance agent, who was able to resolve the problem within a few hours.

Apparently, despite the fact that I had secured and continued to pay for the appropriate amount of insurance for my townhouse, my current mortgage company had no record of my ever having insurance.

Even though you would have thought this would have caused the mortgage company concern far sooner (after all, it was my responsibility to protect its financial best interests), apparently The Seven-Year Glitch finally became an itch that had to be scratched because my mortgage was flagged for a pending interest rate adjustment (and you know that the adjustment isn't going to make my payment amount decrease).

The root cause of the problem was that, in a practice common in the United States, my mortgage was sold (and without my having any say in the matter) by my original lender within the first few months after I purchased my townhouse.

Therefore, my current mortgage company had to integrate my acquired data into its systems. Since my billing data seemed to have been successfully integrated (not only was I receiving my mortgage bills from the new lender, but my property taxes were being paid via my new lender as well), I just assumed that everything was fine.

After all, the recent (and threatening) letters were the only nonbilling correspondence I had received from my current mortgage company in seven years. But one critical piece of data got lost in the acquisition—my insurance information. As I said, my insurance agent was able to resolve the problem within a few hours.

> I can't help but wonder if it will take the mortgage company another seven years to realize that it will soon no longer be my mortgage company.

Then a few days later, I received another letter from my current mortgage company. This letter quite cheerily informed me that I should contact its insurance company if I needed any further assistance from them.

The mortgage company would be happy to explain its many excellent insurance products that I'd be sure to find more than competitive with my current insurance provider. (Apparently, that $2,000 USD a month insurance policy wasn't the only product that it offered in its extensive portfolio.)

I can't help but wonder if it will take the mortgage company another seven years to realize that it will soon no longer be my mortgage company.

Idea 6: The Indian and the Arrow
Phil Simon

When asked recently about his new putter a few hours before teeing off before a Sunday round, baby-faced professional golfer Matt Kuchar responded, "It's usually the Indian, not the arrow."

One could write a book about that statement.

In golf, it's misplaced to blame your poor performance exclusively on your clubs because they don't swing themselves. Of course, that doesn't stop many hacks from doing it, especially after a second ball flies into the woods. Golf companies spend tens of millions of dollars annually convincing 25 handicaps that they can radically transform their games by buying the latest and most expensive clubs. In actuality, the clubs don't matter nearly as much as the person doing the swinging. Give me Phil Mickelson's top-of-the-line irons, and I certainly won't be breaking 70 anytime soon. I'm just not that good.

The same holds true in the enterprise software space. Sure, it's entirely unreasonable to expect people to track their sales of their best customers on pen and paper. I've never seen anyone in a large organization manually writing journal entries in an old-school ledger. Five years ago, however, I worked at one organization that wrote manual checks with a corporate checkbook. (Hey, HR and payroll are often the last to get with the program, right?)

> Buying powerful enterprise resource planning (ERP) and customer relationship management (CRM) systems can certainly yield significant benefits and savings, especially when the organization had been on the right of the technology adoption life cycle.

SIMON SAYS

Buying powerful enterprise resource planning (ERP) and customer relationship management (CRM) systems can certainly yield significant benefits and savings, especially when the organization had been on the right of the technology adoption life cycle. The same holds true for data quality applications. There's absolutely no doubt in my mind that many organizations would benefit from buying them. I'm hard-pressed to think of a more underserved area of IT. But buying them is not the same as deploying them effectively and ensuring that employees use them in ways that make sense.

There's no difference between enterprise software and sporting equipment. Yes, the "best" of each can help, but it all comes back to the Indian and the arrow. How you use either is paramount to what you're using.

Idea 7: Telephone Tag: Bandwidth, Content Detail Records, Data Quality, and a Business Model
David Loshin

I was noodling on a recent experience with a telemarketer using a well-crafted script employing careful ambiguities used to coerce nonthinkers into allowing their telecommunications services to be slammed, as they say. But once I was already preoccupied with the thought process, I started to do a little reading.

One thing the telemarketer said was that the company had an "interconnection agreement" with Verizon, so I went to the Internet (aka the source of all knowledge) and searched for "interconnection agreement." One of the results, the Wikipedia page for "Interconnect Agreement," had an interesting set of comments:

- An "interconnect agreement invariably involves settlement fees based on call source and destination, connection times and duration."
- "On the Internet … the concept of a 'call' is generally hard to define."

Of course, these two statements ping-ponged in my head to lead to a more basic question: what is a "telephone call"?

Actually, as with many commonly used phrases, the term itself is becoming somewhat of an anachronism. Again, Wikipedia provides a little bit of information: "A phone call is a connection over a telephone network between the calling party and the called party." Today we might use a variety of devices and networks to establish a "phone call." (Is a Skype call a phone call?) Calls are documented using a concept called a call detail record (CDR), which contains the details associated with one of these connections, including the calling party, the receiving party, the start time, the duration, as well as a lot of other information that is to be used for billing.

This data is even more important in the context of the interconnection agreement, especially because the myriad calls made under the interconnection agreements have to be invoiced back to the appropriate companies under each agreement. More simply, if I provide service through

> When you charge me for a certain amount of bandwidth, how do I know that the amount you are billing me for is correct?

your network, you need to tell me what I owe you for using your network.

This is where data quality becomes a real issue: validating invoice statements against CDRs. In other words, when you charge me for a certain amount of bandwidth, how do I know that the amount you are billing me for is correct? To validate these numbers, you would need to verify aggregation against the raw data. And then if there are discrepancies between my calculations and yours, then what?

Basically, you need a third party to arbitrate by taking the raw data and the invoices and then independently qualifying the data and resulting invoices and reporting back to both parties. This scenario is not unusual, and fundamentally it's an example of a business model that is almost purely based on data quality management.

Idea 8: Enterprise Information Management—Again
Joyce Norris-Montanari

Enterprise information management, or EIM, is getting more attention by the chief information officers (CIOs) of corporations. A few years ago some companies took on an EIM initiative, and then, somewhere along the line, it was decided that they had a master data management (MDM) or data governance issue. Guess what? You need both to be successful with EIM.

EIM is defined as a segment of interest in the IT area. It specializes in finding solutions for optimal use of information within organizations, such as to support corporate decisions that require the availability of data and

> The objective is to overcome traditional IT issues and manage information for the enterprise at that level.

information (tactical and strategic information). The objective is to overcome traditional IT issues and manage information for the enterprise at that level.

To achieve a euphoric state of EIM, you must consider the following:
- Corporate EIM leadership and buy-in
- Creation of a system and data inventory, which includes data models and metadata
- A sustainable data governance program
- An MDM implementation or initiative

- Management metrics identified to report and identify data performance and usage
- Metadata used as part of every IT solution or initiative
- Cost-effective management for all the above

I started my IT career as a data person thinking at the enterprise level, and I think I will end it there, too. Many data management professionals have tiptoed around the EIM term for years. My customers are demanding that I address data at an enterprise level. I'm tired of tiptoeing and plan to put in my whole foot! How about you?

Idea 9: Eternal September and Tacit Knowledge
Jim Harris

In "Building for the Future" (see Idea 35), Dylan Jones discusses how many organizations are not locking in the knowledge gained on data-driven projects.

This is especially true whenever a data quality initiative is executed as a one-time project and not a sustained program.

When the project team disbands without at least conducting a postmortem to capture lessons learned, its success (or failure, which is often just as beneficial) is not shared with the entire enterprise.

This is a perennial problem—and one not just limited to data quality and other data-driven initiatives—faced by organizations of every size and within every industry, which I refer to as the challenges of Eternal September and Tacit Knowledge.

ETERNAL SEPTEMBER
For most colleges and universities, September is the beginning of the academic year, marked by the arrival of a new freshman class requiring orientation. In the early days of the Internet, this also meant a group of new users unfamiliar with the principles of proper netiquette.

When the Internet's meteoric rise in popularity began to produce endless waves of new users all throughout the year, the term Eternal September was coined to describe this effect, which persists to the present day (and into the foreseeable future).

However, Eternal September is not just an Internet phenomenon.

The training programs included in new employee orientation are common examples of this same effect occurring within organizations.

Another is the new project orientation described by Dylan Jones, where the previous techniques are not being shared, so every new project has to reinvent the wheel. Not only does this add needless time and effort to new initiatives, but without sharing lessons learned, the same costly mistakes are made over and over again.

TACIT KNOWLEDGE

At a very high level, there are two broad categories of knowledge: explicit and tacit.

Explicit knowledge is easily transferable to others in either verbal or written form, which is often easily understood without extensive explanation.

Tacit knowledge is not only difficult to transfer to others, but often not easily recognizable by those who possess it.

Tacit knowledge is often trapped within the minds of data stewards, business analysts, and other subject matter experts (SMEs), who often find it challenging to formalize it into a document or other means that can be easily shared with and understood by others lacking their extensive experience.

> Some lessons in both our professional and our personal lives cannot be taught; they can only be learned.

Experience is popularly believed to be the path that separates explicit knowledge from tacit knowledge, which could alternatively be defined as wisdom.

Some lessons in both our professional and our personal lives cannot be taught; they can only be learned. Borrowing the sage words of Marcel Proust:

> We do not receive wisdom, we must discover it for ourselves, after a journey through the wilderness, which no one can make for us, which no one can spare us, for our wisdom is the point of view from which we come at last to regard the world.

YOUR ORGANIZATION'S VIEW OF THE WORLD

Although the risks of Eternal September can be mitigated with diligence and dedication, the challenge of formalizing your organization's tacit knowledge is more daunting.

Comprehensive documentation, especially distributed via a Wiki, SharePoint folders, or some other information sharing portal, can conquer (or at least greatly reduce the effects of) Eternal September, which is fundamentally concerned with sharing explicit knowledge. However, this approach is often far less effective with tacit knowledge.

Idea 10: Baseball, George Costanza, and the Problem with Unwritten Rules

Phil Simon

It's one of those things that many learned baseball folks don't understand: what are the unwritten rules of baseball? We know that you're not supposed to try to add to a 10-run lead in the top of the ninth inning. Sure, that's a given. But what about trying to come back from a 10-run deficit in the bottom of the fourth? Evidently, that's a no-no as well, as we learned on September 1, 2010 in a game between the Washington Nationals and the Florida Marlins.

The question becomes: where do you draw the line? No one really knows, as evinced by the fight in that game between Washington's Nyler Morgan and Marlins' pitcher Chris Volstad. Beaning a guy once is acceptable, but throwing behind him (even if that guy took out your catcher last time) is prohibited.

Now, I'm no baseball nut (at least anymore), but I often do find gray areas such as these vexing. More important to this forum, I find them to be interesting parallels to the data quality and management worlds in which many of us spend so much time.

UNWRITTEN RULES

The problem with unwritten rules in a data management context is just that: they're unwritten. It's entirely possible, even probable, that someone doesn't know about a key policy or procedure until it's too late. Sure, you can lock down applications, tables, records, systems, and networks with different security options. That's not to say that mistakes can't happen by sheer ignorance.

Mistakes may also take the form of miscommunication or misunderstanding by skilled end users. I'll cop to this one right now. A few years ago, I was tasked with making about 400 changes to employee records, manually syncing two disparate systems. (Trust me…I tried to automate this, but it just wasn't possible.) A director explained to me what she wanted me to do and I understood her instructions—or so I thought.

> The problem with unwritten rules in a data management context is just that: they're unwritten.

As it turned out, there was a minor but key piece that I didn't completely understand, causing me to make some mistakes. Nothing was destroyed, but it took me about a day to make the fixes.

SIMON SAYS

No one says that everything needs to be codified in the workplace with data management—or anything else. I am reminded of the *Seinfeld* episode "The Red Dot," in which George sleeps with a cleaning woman at work.

> **BOSS:** I'm going to get right to the point. It has come to my attention that you and the cleaning woman have engaged in sexual intercourse on the desk in your office. Is that correct?
>
> **GEORGE:** Who said that?
>
> **BOSS:** She did.
>
> **GEORGE:** Was that wrong? Should I have not done that? I tell you I gotta plead ignorance on this thing because if anyone had said anything to me at all when I first started here that that sort of thing was frowned upon, you know, cause I've worked in a lot of offices and I tell you people do that all the time.[1]

There has to be a happy medium in any organization with regard to written versus unwritten rules. Too many of the former leads to excessive

---

1. Jason Alexander (George) has said before that this is his favorite scene of the entire series.

bureaucracy, inertia, and an inability to respond quickly to key developments. Too many of the latter means systematic chaos, pure and simple.

Idea 11: When the Integration Project Is Not So Integrated

Joyce Norris-Montanari

Has this ever happened to you? You think you're working on integrating a few systems together onto one nice platform for reporting and disseminating information to the enterprise, and then you find out the plan is to *not* really integrate the data? It happens to me a lot!

For an integration project, I'd perform the following tasks:

- Talk with the business users to see what works and what doesn't work in the current environment. I'd look for enhancements and items that may not be needed anymore. For example, maybe the business users no longer use some data or reports.

> Talk with the business users to see what works and what doesn't work in the current environment.

- Analyze the systems to be integrated by documenting the input/output interfaces, inventory the infrastructure, and inventory the database objects. To analyze the database objects, I would reverse-engineer the database into a data modeling tool and look at the structural information. I would profile the data from all the systems to analyze the integration points, looking for outliers and data that won't integrate based on data types.
- Analyze the existing reports for any commonalities, and design the end reporting environment.
- Prioritize which portions of the system(s) should be moved to the new platform first (in an integrated database, of course).
- Develop the interfaces and reports. Then I would prototype with the business user.

- Integrate the data on paper and in the database using ETL tools where possible.
- Implement and test.
- Audit and monitor.

Maybe my issue is management dissemination of information, not the rest of the team. That's another subject for another day!

Idea 12: Data Quality Chinese Whispers
Dylan Jones

When starting out with a roadmap to improve data quality, people often face the challenge of where to begin. Your team may be inexperienced in creating things like data quality scorecards and assessment metrics to reliably gauge the best starting point.

When faced with this issue, I often advise looking at information chains that align with your most critical service value chains. Within these chains are numerous information junction points where data must flow across the boundary. These can be between different departments, different systems, and even different customers.

Whenever we move data from one environment to another, we create a form of Chinese whispers.

One side of the data junction can misinterpret the meaning of the data or make subtle changes, which can lead to defects. This defective data then flows into further downstream recipients until eventually the data can look very different from the original source.

I operate a great deal in the telecoms space, and this issue is common. The service chains can be incredibly complex; as a result, the corresponding information chains can span multiple systems and teams, even for the most basic of service requests.

The planning department may request a new piece of equipment to be provisioned, so a new record is created. This may be passed to the installation team, which moves into action and builds the infrastructure. The team updates its records and passes on details to the network team, which now can channel traffic through the installed assets. The service maintenance team may take a feed of the data to ensure that it can automate a service schedule based on the service levels of the inventory in question.

Each department has a subtly different use of the data, which can lead to large discrepancies. For example, in one telecom company, I found 500 equipment-naming conventions in one system, but by the time the data had travelled through three downstream systems, the conventions had risen to more than 7,000!

For the data quality practitioner, the type of data quality defects that these interface issues can create results in a gold mine of opportunities, such as these:

- Reinstatement or decommissioning of stranded assets
- Online assets being charged to new accounts
- Reduction in new equipment purchases
- Reduction in service maintenance fees
- More profitable use of physical floor space

In conclusion, if you're starting a data quality initiative, it can be extremely beneficial to map some of the critical information chains in your business. Highlight the main data interfaces between business functions/systems, and then begin your data quality assessment by comparing data across the interface.

> If you're starting a data quality initiative, it can be extremely beneficial to map some of the critical information chains in your business.

There is always low-hanging fruit, ripe for the picking, in these types of situations.

Idea 13: The Fiscal Calendar Effect
Jim Harris

I wrote about Eternal September in Idea 9. It's just one of many calendar effects, which are changes in behavior that appear to be related to changes on the calendar. Calendar effects are sometimes referred to as seasonal tendencies. Although they can have other contexts, they're mostly discussed in an economic context, such as their effects on stock markets and retail prices.

For the purposes of this Idea, I want to focus on the Fiscal Calendar Effect—specifically, how it affects enterprise information initiatives.

THE FISCAL CALENDAR EFFECT

In the United States, the fiscal year is divided into four fiscal quarters which, most commonly, are aligned with the calendar year. In other words:

- Q1 = January–March
- Q2 = April–June
- Q3 = July–September
- Q4 = October–December

And in the United States, the majority of organizations, both public and private, are extremely fiscal quarter-oriented in their planning and execution.

The Business and Society Program at the Aspen Institute, which I first read about in the book *Switch* by Chip Heath and Dan Heath, is committed to fighting what it refers to as "short-termism" in the business world, which refers to organizations with a short-term focus that can't afford to tackle long-term problems.

As the CEO of a huge financial services firm was anonymously quoted while pointing to the 90-day calendar posted on his wall: "That is my reality."

No one is trying to demonize executive management. The fact is that although most executives would probably prefer, all things being equal, to have a longer-term focus, the culture of the stock market encourages short-term thinking.

The limited planning and execution stranglehold of fiscal quarter orientation, especially within publicly traded companies, is the practice—not required by any law—of what the Heaths refer to as "the bizarre Kabuki dance of earnings guidance."

Each fiscal quarter, "a public company sets expectations for the earnings per share it will deliver in its next quarterly financial report. Then, when the company files its report, a miracle occurs—the company announces that it beat the expectations!"

This Kabuki dance creates the Fiscal Calendar Effect, which often creates dead zones in the planning and execution of enterprise information initiatives.

In other words, after the planning and earnings guidance for the next fiscal quarter has been finalized, if your project—or the next phase of your program—didn't make the cut, you know that for the next 90 days no substantial progress can be made.

Additionally, the Fiscal Calendar Effect can alter the priorities of approved projects and program phases. If the quarterly financial report is not forecasted to be positive, previously approved efforts for the current quarter can be abruptly halted—and not necessarily deferred to the next fiscal quarter.

THE FISCAL CALENDAR EFFECT ON YOUR ORGANIZATION

Enterprise information initiatives are sensitive to disruptions in their momentum.

The morale of the employees working on these initiatives can be negatively affected, especially when they're given no insight into why these disruptions occur.

In addition, the enterprise-wide collaboration required by these initiatives is often difficult enough to initiate. So when the next phase is delayed, deferred, or even canceled, it can send the signal that the collaboration wasn't worth the effort.

> Enterprise information initiatives are sensitive to disruptions in their momentum.

This effect can be quite similar to when employees working for a public company read the press releases about the great year the organization has been having financially but then learn that their year-end bonuses are being reduced, deferred, or eliminated.

Although I understand that honest feedback on this question is probably classified as MGMF ("might get me fired"), how does the Fiscal Calendar Effect affect the planning and execution of enterprise information initiatives at your organization?

Idea 14: Need-to-Know Data

Joyce Norris-Montanari

When companies collect and store information about their customers, they follow no code of conduct. There's no standard. There's nothing that safeguards privacy and establishes rules of the road.

The government is trying to include some guidelines or rules around this information, but here is an example:

A friend who works in human resources (HR) sent me an email that said, "Look what they know about you." Sure enough, the website that the HR group used had more information about me than I wanted anyone to know. Granted, in my earlier career, I was an instructor at The Data Warehousing Institute (TDWI), contributed to lots of articles, and so on. Basically, my information was accessible.

Here are some questions and what-ifs for you to consider:

- What if my credit score is not correct and I can't refinance my house?
- What if my address is incorrect?
- What if I don't have children, but children's names are listed?
- What if I got divorced a long time ago, and my ex is still listed? What if he had a shady past?

A long time ago when this happened to a friend of mine and he couldn't get a car loan, we went through the steps to correct the data. (The credit bureaus listed him as married, with four kids, living in California, and having defaulted on a previous mortgage. In truth, he was single, childless, living in Colorado, and had never owned a house, let alone defaulted on one.)

As a society, we have created the same web of incorrect public information that many organizations have created with their internal data.

Now let's move on to how information is used.

My husband took his laptop to Cozumel, Mexico, the last time we went for some relaxation. One afternoon when I was waiting for him to come back from a dive trip, I logged onto Facebook to see what my friends, colleagues, and grandchildren were doing. Because I had logged on in Mexico, all the ads launched by Facebook showed up in Spanish.

Facebook was trying to integrate certain types of data about me to re-target me for marketing campaigns.

> Assumptions made...are not always accurate.

Data mining, data integration, and targeted marketing campaigns are pretty hot on the Internet. They are picking up information about every transaction being made. Obviously, the assumptions made from that information are not always accurate—not everyone logging on from Mexico speaks Spanish. Keep trying, guys—catch me if you can!

Idea 15: Mastering Product Data
David Loshin

Product data is quirky and different from party data. Product data sets and names contain descriptive information, yet they are eminently parsable and can be mapped to a normalized form. This means that product data is nicely suited to MDM. In essence, a master product directory can be used as a standard index for parsed and standardized product names.

Profiling, parsing, and standardization are key components of the process. At the start, profiling can be used to analyze string patterns and recognize commonly used abbreviations and acronyms. Once those terms are recognized and evaluated for meaning, parsing and standardization rules can be defined to recognize the individual terms, map them to a standard form, and then normalize the representation in preparation for matching against a product master. In other words, the same process typically executed for party name matching can be applied to product name matching, with the only difference being a limit to the ways that errors are embedded within the strings.

> A product master index might be a lot simpler than a party master index, and it might be more useful when the product name data can be used for more than just identification.

In turn, a product master index might be a lot simpler than a party master index, and it might be more useful when the product name data can be used for more than just identification. Because the name carries the description, it can also be used for classification. In other words, not only can you match the name of a product, you can use its name to determine what kind of a product it is.

Idea 16: *Heat* and Trust
Phil Simon

One of my all-time favorite movies is *Heat*. Directed by Michael Mann, *Heat* is the story of a master criminal and master cop played by two actors you might know: Robert DeNiro and Al Pacino.

In perhaps the most famous scene in the movie, the two meet on screen at a coffee shop. They feel each other out, realizing that they have a great deal in common even though their professions are polar opposites.

One line from this scene has always resonated with me:

NEIL (DeNiro): You must have worked some (@#%&!) crews.

VINCENT (Pacino): I worked all kinds.

You're probably thinking right about now, "That's great, Phil, but I really don't care about obscure quotes from your favorite flicks." Fair enough, but there was a point to this little diversion.

ALL KINDS

While my writing has picked up over the past six months, I continue to make most of my money via consulting. Like many consultants, sometimes I get to work with organizations that do things the right way. Of course, I also work with organizations that seem hell-bent on making things as difficult as possible and maximizing their chance at failure. In other words, to channel my inner Pacino, "I worked all kinds."

My last two projects couldn't have been more different. To say that my last gig was challenging is the acme of understatement. I still believe I'll see the inside of a courtroom at some point because of it. Given that, I knew that my next assignment would be considerably less difficult. It was. (This reminds me of the time that I shot a 117 at Warrenbrook.[2] I knew that my next round there would be better. It was. I shot a completely legitimate 87. Golf applause.)

TRUST

So, what's the main difference between my last two projects, other than my stress level? In a word, trust. My current client has always trusted consultants, whereas my previous one never did.

Good consultants (attempt to) steer the ship, but the very best ones rely heavily on their crew members. To continue with the metaphor, a project may be the equivalent of smooth sailing at the beginning. Everyone wants the same thing:

- A successful implementation at or under budget
- The product delivered on schedule
- Desired functionality
- No headaches

REQUIREMENTS FOR CLIENTS AND CONSULTANTS

Consultants should not only focus on life at 30,000 feet. Those who do are remiss. At the same time, however, they should not micromanage and unnecessarily involve themselves in every day-to-day issue. Good consultants know how to strike a balance and roll up their sleeves when necessary.

For their part, clients need to do the following throughout data migration projects:

> Consultants should not only focus on life at 30,000 feet.

- Listen to consultants when they bring issues to light
- Proactively approach consultants to ensure that individual and organizational objectives are on track
- Broach issues to consultants as needed

SIMON SAYS

Obviously, there's a great deal more to say about the client-consultant relationship. My main point here is that most data migration and IT projects

---

2. A short, narrow, and tough little course in New Jersey.

probably won't be successful without a high degree of trust between consultants and clients. We each bring something to the table:

- Consultants know a great deal about how other companies do things. We're good with tools.
- Client end users know a great deal about how they do things. They know process.

Most data migration and IT projects probably won't be successful without a high degree of trust between consultants and clients.

It's equally foolish to expect a consultant to immediately know the ins and outs of a new client. Similarly, consultants shouldn't expect their new clients to know industry or application best practices. While the outcome of no IT project is guaranteed, good things do happen by trusting each other.

Idea 17: Know Your Audience
Rich Murnane

Like kids on Christmas morning, almost immediately after receiving and installing our favorite data quality tool at our shop, we went wild and started cleansing data like crazy. After the indulgence of all this data cleansing (a data cleansing hangover?), we decided we would take a breather and spend some cycles building metrics about our data. Yes, we should have done this first, but we needed to get some data cleaned up, and we needed to do it fast. Once our framework for capturing data about our clients' data quality was designed and implemented, we decided we would represent these metrics as numeric values called data quality scores.

After some deep thought and significant effort, we were finally ready to communicate these data quality scores for clients to our senior management. We put together some reports and graphics, met with our senior managers, and, sure enough, we were completely surprised when the fruits of our labor were met with disdain.

What did we do wrong? Something so simple it's almost embarrassing. We didn't know our audience. Our audience was composed of senior executives, and the senior executives at our shop like to hear good news, not bad news. The delivery of our message and associated data quality scores was completely backward because we focused only on the negative. Figure 2 shows the right and wrong approaches to these data quality scores.

Data Quality Scores - the wrong direction				
	October	November	December	
Client X	9	10	11	UP should
Client Y	5	5	5	be good,
Client Z	11	10	9	but it's not here!

Data Quality Scores - the right direction				
	October	November	December	
Client X	91	90	89	
Client Y	95	95	95	
Client Z	89	90	91	UP is good!

Figure 2: Data Quality Scores

We walked into the meeting with reports saying things like, "9 percent of client X's data has issues," but we should have been saying, "91 percent of client X's data is error-free." Our graphs should have indicated that our data quality scores went up when things were better, but they didn't; they went down. Although mathematically our graphs were correct, the executives at our company like to think positive. Graphically speaking, they think "up is good," so our message and our graphs were going the wrong direction (see Figures 3 and 4 on page 27).

Now, I'm not saying that we couldn't explain our way out of this, nor am I saying that metrics or measurements should always go up, but as data quality professionals, we tend to focus on the negative way too often. Had we changed our communication strategy a little bit, our hard work and cool graphs would have been much better received. In your data quality efforts, I'd strongly recommend focusing on the positive; when in doubt, remember that up is good.

> As data quality professionals, we tend to focus on the negative way too often.

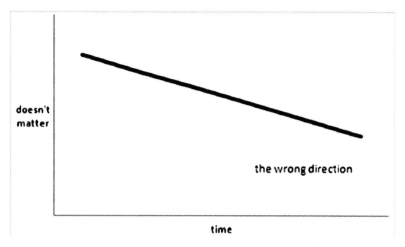

Figure 3: Down Is Bad: Executive Perception, 1

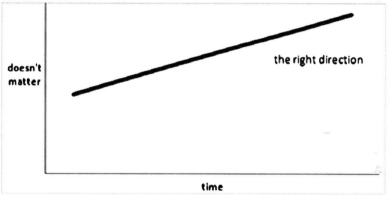

Figure 4: Up Is Good: Executive Perception, 2

Idea 18: Integrating Data in the Enterprise

Joyce Norris-Montanari

The other day, I was chatting with one of the enterprise architects at my client's about integrating corporate data. This company has acquired other companies, which had already acquired other companies. Get the picture? Anyway, we wanted to create an enterprise data architecture that made sense for this client.

So, how should we (the team) handle this situation?

1. We are trying to list data by source system. We identify the type of data, specify any interfaces (in and out), and then categorize it within a subject area. Subject area in this case refers to customer data, financial data, or product data. This is actually difficult to accomplish because

> After we have a good handle on where we're going and where we've been, we can start to profile the data for quality issues *before* we migrate.

there are so many source systems. For example, the call center alone has more than 15. This step also requires an understanding of what source systems are going away during system migrations and consolidation efforts.

2. As we gather the information listed in step 1, we can start designing and defining a subject area diagram. This gives us an enterprise perspective of the data categories that we are working with during this exercise. From the subject area diagram and the source system analysis (step 1), we can assist upper management with information to plan a data and consolidation plan.

3. After we have a good handle on where we're going and where we've been, we can start to profile the data for quality issues *before* we migrate.

Idea 19: When Is a Person Not a Person?
David Loshin

When is a person not a person? When that person is more than one person.

Here is at least one form of the scenario. My wife and I share the same loyalty card at our local supermarket. All the data associated with customer interactions is logged in association with one customer identifier, no matter which of us does the shopping. Yet when my wife goes to the store, her shopping cart probably looks a little different from when I do the shopping. So the question becomes: what characteristics can be used to differentiate the different customer facets even when there is only one customer record? An example of the value of answering this question accurately is real-time offers, such as texting a coupon for a specific up-sell or cross-sell opportunity to one of our mobile phones.

> What characteristics can be used to differentiate the different customer facets even when there is only one customer record?

This is actually not a rare situation because it happens whenever a representative of a household acts on behalf of different individuals in the household. Other examples? Everyone in our family uses the same library card to borrow books. I do all the online ordering, whether it is for technical books, handheld games, or baby CDs. Other examples are shared bank accounts, credit cards, and charitable donations.

Essentially, this is no longer a question of record linkage, but of entity disambiguation. This is closely related to the linkage problem. But instead of emphasizing the weights on the data elements that have wide value variation, we have to ask what variables distinguish behavior. Interestingly, we end up reducing the weight on a strong identifying attribute such as customer identifier while emphasizing those attributes that tend to slight variation.

I think there is an interesting application here, even though I haven't really thought this through 100 percent. I suspect there are other areas of analysis that address the same problem, yet I wonder whether this is basically the reciprocal operation of matching and might become an integral part of future data quality tools and technology.

Idea 20: Is Security Inhibiting Your Data Quality?
Phil Simon

I was reminded recently of an incident that happened to me a few years ago. I'll recount it here for the explicit purpose of raising what I believe is a key data quality–related issue: can excessive security inhibit data quality?

Three years ago, I worked for an organization in the midst of a major ERP application upgrade, the details of which aren't terribly interesting. As a lazy and cost-conscious consultant, I proposed working remotely much of the time to minimize project costs. Everyone agreed, and I soon received instructions for how to log in to the organization's virtual private network (VPN).

> Can excessive security inhibit data quality?

Let's just say that said instructions were anything but simple, as evinced by the fact it took 15 pages to explain the process. The term "amazingly complex" comes to mind. Trying to log in crashed my computer twice, and I'm talking blue screen of death here.

Wow.

Although it was easier to log in while onsite (as many employees were), strict measures surrounding system time-outs and reauthentication requirements meant that simply doing one's job was no easy task. As a result, many employees opted to keep key information in easily accessed standalone databases and spreadsheets, not in the enterprise system. What's more, errors in the ERP system often remained unfixed because they were simply too cumbersome to fix.

The results of this overly secure environment:

- Rampant data quality issues
- Inaccurate reporting
- Suboptimal decisions

FUNDAMENTAL QUESTIONS

As I thought about that client experience, a few questions popped into my hyperkinetic mind:

- What's the right or optimal amount of security in an organization?
- What are the data quality and management issues related to too much security?
- What about too little security?
- Is too safe better than not safe enough?

SIMON SAYS

I don't have all the answers to these admittedly lofty questions. Being at my core a consultant, the answer of course is, "It depends." Type of industry, regulatory requirements, use of clouds, and type of systems are but a few of the many factors that drive CIO decisions to secure their enterprises in specific ways.

But if you make things too safe, aren't you inviting end user excuses such as, "But it's too hard?" Is one of the costs of excessive security poor data quality and management?

Idea 21: "If Not Now, When? And If Not You, Who?"
Dylan Jones

I was reading an old post by Jill Dyché recently titled "The Tyranny of Consensus."[i]

I love reading her blog because there is a great take-away from every post, and this one doesn't disappoint. The last sentence should be stapled to the wall of anyone who has the ability to improve the quality of data: "If not now, when? And if not you, who?"

It neatly sums up two fundamental issues that many organizations face regarding data quality: those old foes procrastination and accountability.

The topic of procrastination came home to me again recently after speaking with one organization that was in the process of completing a data migration/consolidation into a new CRM system. I asked the question: when will the program kick off to maintain the required levels of data quality in the new system?

The answer was all too common: nothing is planned.

Despite investing several million dollars in a completely new data and

> Without a continuous program of measurement, monitoring, and improvement, the data is guaranteed to degrade in quality over time.

service architecture, there was nothing scheduled to ensure that the data would be fit for purpose over the coming years.

On paper, collapsing multiple customer systems into one customer hub makes great data quality sense—now the entire organization can have a single access point, right? Yes, absolutely, but you now have the added problem of multiple departments creating and updating the same customer master data. Without a continuous program of measurement, monitoring, and improvement, the data is guaranteed to degrade in quality over time. It's a statistical certainty.

If there was no initiative planned, when would it take place? Tomorrow? Next year?

I then asked the question: is there a likely sponsor or data stakeholder who will step up and take charge of data quality into the future?

Again, the answer was all too common: no one.

By removing the legacy satellite systems (that each had a data owner) and consolidating into one environment, the organization is effectively splitting the ownership of the subject area data across multiple lines of business: operations, sales, billing, and marketing. Without a data governance framework to clarify and orchestrate the necessary policies and rules of data quality engagement, the new data landscape will begin to fall foul of SEP (Somebody Else's Problem) Syndrome. (Thanks to Julian Schwarzenbach for this timely acronym.)

If you are in any way responsible for data, there are always ways to improve. There are myriad free and low-cost, simple activities that, when implemented, cumulatively can make a significant impact on quality levels.

You can pay a little right now, today, or you can pay a lot more in the future when the new ERP system launch date comes and goes due to poor quality data or the regulator loses trust in your revenue accounting figures.

The same is true with accountability. The principles of data governance are not rocket science. They require people to care about the data enough to plan for the future, to halt the inevitable decay that time will surely inflict on data.

If not now, when? And if not you, who?

Two simple questions, but the answers will speak volumes about where your organization's real data quality motivations lie.

Idea 22: How Joyce Saved Christmas
Joyce Norris-Montanari

I visited Santa at the local shopping center the other day. I figured, why not get my turn with the jolly old elf? So I waited in line with all the small children to sit on his lap and talk about what I wanted for Christmas. I walked up there, sat down, and said to Santa, "Let's talk data." He said he didn't have data issues, and I replied, "I think you do."

Here's what I think:

- How does Santa know if it's Joyce A. Norris, Joyce Norris-Montanari, Joyce Montanari, Joyce A. Norris-Montanari, or any other versions of my name who wants Wii-Dance II? Is he going to get a copy for all of us? How will he tag which one of my names has been naughty and which one has been nice? Without an integrated list using clustering, how would he know that all those versions are really me? After he gets a good integrated list, he could decide if I was naughty or nice. (For those who know me: no input required here!)

> Without an integrated list using clustering, how would he know that all those versions are really me?

- Santa's crew of elves may not be quite as skilled at data integration and cleansing as the rest of us. So I offered to run some data profiling against his list for him. We looked for incomplete addresses and fixed them right up with our data quality software. We also set up a clustering algorithm (with some software) that clustered all best "Joyce" information for his list.

I sure hope I get what I asked for. Well, I guess I have done my job to save Christmas this year!

Idea 23: Hybrids
Phil Simon

Many of us have seen firsthand how business and IT folks often speak vastly different languages. I call this the technical-functional disconnect, and it has plagued many organizations, projects, and people. The bottom line is simply that when some say tomato, others hear coconut.

Enter the hybrid. (Disclaimer: I firmly define myself as a hybrid.) We hybrids are a rare species in most organizations. Hybrids adeptly bridge the IT-business chasm, often acting as interpreters. They know enough about what the business wants to frame those requests in terms that IT can easily understand and synthesize.

> Many of us have seen first-hand how business and IT folks often speak vastly different languages.

By the same token, they know enough about back-end things (read: databases, tables, interdependencies) that they can stop a runaway business end user from making life a living hell for the IT department—and the organization in general.

There's great value in hybrids—for both the organization employing/contracting them and the hybrids themselves. Companies often get a "two-for-one" deal, and individuals can usually earn more money. For our part, we hybrids also make ourselves lynchpins, capable of withstanding rounds of layoffs.

The stereotypical developer has no idea about the difference between a debit and a credit. Most business folks might not know about data profiling or MDM. We tend to know what we know. Those of us with curiosity to expand our knowledge bases are often interrupted by pointless meetings, excessive emails, and other office distractions. Author Jason Fried made this point at a recent TED conference.[ii]

But this lack of knowledge can be dangerous. After all, when you think about most business problems, how many are purely technical? *Purely* functional? Not too many fall squarely into one category, in my admittedly jaundiced experience. When solving the majority of problems, I almost always have had to concurrently put on my technical and business hats.

SIMON SAYS

I understand the need to keep costs down, especially in current economic times. By obsessing over costs, however, aren't many organizations missing a tremendous opportunity to augment their staff with extremely valuable individuals? I just don't understand why many chief executive officers (CXOs) of large organizations fail to recognize the value of those with equal parts depth and breadth.

Yes, it's important to know SQL code if you're a database administrator (DBA). Marketing folks need to understand the ins and outs of market segmentation, lest their organizations lose market share. But there exists between these two groups a vast netherworld. Why not try to bridge it?

Part II:
Data Quality

Few people would disagree about the critical importance of data quality. Yet, organizations continue to struggle mightily with data quality issues, incurring additional risk and making suboptimal decisions in this process. Data quality remains much easier said than done. What's more, without sufficient data quality, how can an organization become more mature with respect to its data management? How can it embrace data governance without adequate data quality?

The contributors chime in with ideas on how to improve the quality of information in organizational systems, applications, and databases.

Idea 24: Predictably Poor Data Quality
Jim Harris

For decades, data quality experts have been telling us that poor quality is bad for our data, bad for our decisions, bad for our business, and just plain all around bad, bad, bad. Did I already mention it's bad?

So why does poor data quality continue to exist and persist?

Have the experts been all talk, but with no plan for taking action? Have the technology vendors not been evolving their data quality tools to become more powerful, easier to use, and more aligned with the business processes that create data and the technical architectures that manage data?

Have the business schools been unleashing morons into the workforce who can't design a business process correctly? Have employees been intentionally corrupting data in an attempt to undermine their employers' success? Would any perfectly rational organization suffer from poor data quality?

I recently finished reading the excellent book *Predictably Irrational* by Dan Ariely, the James B. Duke professor of psychology and behavioral economics at Duke University. I am fascinated with behavioral economics, which is a relatively new field combining aspects of both psychology and economics. The basic assumption underlying standard economics is that we will always make rational decisions in our best interest, often justified by a simple cost-benefit analysis.

Behavioral economics more realistically acknowledges that we are not always rational, and, most important, our irrationality is neither random nor senseless; instead, it is quite predictable when the complex psychology of human behavior is considered.

The basic assumption underlying most theories of data quality is that because the business benefits of high-quality data are obvious compared to the detrimental effects of poor qual-

> There are, without question, some data quality problems that are indeed attributable to people problems.

ity, any people, processes, or technology that allows poor data quality must either be acting irrationally or otherwise be somehow defective.

Therefore, preventive measures, once put into place, will correct "the problem" and alleviate any need for future corrective action, such as data cleansing. Everything, and everyone, will then be rational and wonderful in a world of perfect data quality.

THE ROOT CAUSE OF POOR DATA QUALITY

Late last year, in an intentionally provocative blog post[iii], Julian Schwarzenbach declared that there is no such thing as a data quality problem because people are the root cause of all data quality problems.

If we recognized this fact, Julian explained, solving data quality problems would involve solving people problems. Although Julian was partially countering the views of some who believe that technology alone is the solution, there are, without question, some data quality problems that are indeed attributable to people problems.

Julian provided an excellent list exemplifying how a lack of data ownership as well as assuming data quality is someone else's responsibility is the fundamental root case for many data quality problems.

If people can cause poor data quality, how do we correct their behavior?

BEHAVIORAL DATA QUALITY

Whether or not it is a relatively new field, I am using the term behavioral data quality to describe the inclusion of aspects of psychology within the data quality profession.

CONCLUSION

The Upside of Irrationality is the recently published and provocative follow-up book by Dan Ariely. Although I look forward to reading it, I doubt I could make a similar case for the upside of poor data quality.

However, the first book explained the dangers of not testing our intuitions, thinking we can always predict our behavior, and assuming our behavior will always be rational.

Better knowledge of these flawed perspectives can help us better understand the root causes of our predictably poor data quality. Most important, it can help us develop far more effective tactics and strategies for implementing successful and sustainable data quality improvements.

Idea 25: Too Much Club
Phil Simon

Times are tight all over, especially in the banking world. Let's just say that my phone hasn't been ringing off the hook with calls from financial institutions over the past few years. I suspect I'm not alone here. All companies are trying to save money these days. Most that are looking for consultants want to find those with the lowest possible rates. What else is new?

On occasion, a company does the right thing. It focuses on long-term data management, finding the right resource to help it get from point A to point B. This happened to me just a few hours after I returned from DataFlux IDEAS 2010.

A fairly large bank (call it FLB here) in the middle of some significant mergers and acquisitions (M&A) activity needed to find a resource to help move and validate a decent amount of internal data. The company needed that same someone to set up an automated process to continue to do so. At the risk of being immodest, I'm pretty darn good at doing this type of thing. Of course, because of the economy, FLB was looking to keep costs to a minimum. For me, this meant a rate about 50 percent lower than my self-imposed minimum. FLB anticipated that the data migration project would take about seven weeks.

> On data migration projects, all else equal, you're better off having an overqualified consultant capable of doing more than you need.

I initially passed on the job. (A guy's gotta have standards, right?) I explained that I charge what I charge because, although I can make no guarantees, I have found that I can typically bang out work like this in a shorter time period than most. I've stuck to my guns before and lost work because of it. I firmly expected the same to happen here. But then a strange thing happened: I didn't lose the job.

I got the call, nailed the interview, and will start the gig soon. I'm confident that I can do this job, and I'll bet you a Coke that FLB will spend less money on consultants (me), even with my higher rate. I'd be surprised if we're not finished in half of the projected seven weeks. For example, I'll set up an extract, transform, and load (ETL) process for 50,000 records, with additional validation reports. If the amount of data increases by a factor of 10, the changes will be invisible to the end users. I'm building in a crazy amount of slack here.

TOO MUCH CLUB

There's a golfing equivalent to this anecdote. (Of course, there always is, isn't there?) On certain holes, it's better to take too much club. For example, when hitting over water (aka, the drink), it's better to be too long than too short. If you're stuck between a 5-iron (175 yards or so) and a 6 (160, give or take), hit the 5. You don't want to be wet and take a penalty stroke. Hitting "a big 6" means swinging too hard, introducing additional risk.

SIMON SAYS

The data management equivalent is obvious, I hope. On data migration projects, all else equal, you're better off having an overqualified consultant capable of doing more than you need. The same applies to a data migration and validation tool. Finding a smart cookie at half of my rate only capable of handling spreadsheets is penny wise but pound foolish.

In other words, too much club can mean fewer strokes.

Idea 26: Identity Resolution, Cleansing, and Survivorship
David Loshin

When two records have been determined to refer to the same real-world entity, it means that a duplicate version of what should be a unique record has been introduced. Whether it is due to a merging of data sets from different sources or the absence of controls to prevent duplicates from being entered is irrelevant if the business objective is to resolve multiple records into a single representation. The challenge is that, when faced with two (or possibly) more versions of information supposedly representing the same entity, how do you determine which values from which records will be copied over into the unified record?

The answer to this question reflects a philosophical standpoint regarding the question of correcting bad data—namely, whether you should ever delete or overwrite values assumed to be incorrect. From one perspective, inconsistent data will have impacts to the business users downstream, and reducing or eliminating inconsistency leads to improved business processes. From the other perspective, any piece of information is valuable, and deleting one version of a person's name or a product description because it doesn't match another version means the deleted version will be lost. Therefore, in some situations, a "best" record can be created to update all identified duplicates, whereas in other situations, all the values are maintained while the best version can be materialized on demand when requested.

This process of determining the best values is called survivorship. Of course, if all the values are the same, survivorship is not questioned. But when there are variant data values, survivorship decisions must be related to additional measures of quality. These quality measures are a function of three contextual factors: the quality of the data source from which the record comes, the measure of quality of the record (that is, based on defined dimensions), and the quality of the specific values.

- **Quality of the source:** Different data sources exhibit different characteristics in terms of their conformance to business expectations defined using defined data quality dimensions. In general, if a data set is subjected to an assessment and is assigned a quality score, those relative scores become one data point. In other words, given a record from a data set with a high-quality score matched with a record from a data set with a low-quality score, it would be reasonable to select values from the first record over the second when they vary.

  > When there is variation between the two records and the sources are of equal quality, assess the quality of the records, and that will provide the next level of guidance.

- **Quality of the record:** Similarly, each record can be viewed within its own context. Data quality rules can be measured at the record level of granularity (such as completeness of the data elements, consistency across data values, conformance to domain validation constraints, and other reasonableness directives), and these measures can provide a relative assessment of the quality of one record over the other. So when there is variation between the two records and the sources are of equal quality, assess the quality of the records, and that will provide the next level of guidance.

- **Quality of the value:** If the sources are of equal quality and the records are of equal quality, the next level of precision involves the values themselves. The values have some intrinsic dimensions associated with them, such as syntactic consistency, semantic consistency, and domain validity. Here are some additional suggestions for comparing the values pulled from the set of matched records:

  o **Value currency:** Objectively, more recent values can be presumed to be better.

  o **Content "density":** Value strings containing more information might be considered better. A fully spelled-out first name contains more information than just an initial, and that can be presumed to be a better value.

  o **Value frequency:** When multiple records are flagged as potential duplicates, values that appear with higher frequency may be considered more reliable than those that do not.

Of course, these suggestions are relatively subjective; in fact, they may conflict with each other in practice, so it is wise to integrate your decision process with the results of a data quality assessment.

Idea 27: Where the Rubber Meets the Road in Data Quality
Joyce Norris-Montanari

Today was the day that I categorized the calculation for a specific client's change in reporting environment. For years we have said things like this:

- The data design is the most important.

- Don't make the tool overcome a bad design.
- Changing to another reporting tool is no big deal.

Well, it shouldn't be a big deal, but sometimes it is. All we should have to do is the following:

> When the design is not optimal and the quality of the data is suspect, the job is not so easy.

- Inventory all the reports, looking for inactive ones.
- Analyze and document the reports by fact and dimensions.
- Re-create a few reports with the new tool as a prototype.

We must create the new reports, making sure security is in place, there are procedures and disciplines for handling changes to these reports, and change management exists for new reports.

When the design is not optimal and the quality of the data is suspect, the job is not so easy. We may need to consider these options:

- Diving into the SQL for each report and documenting the analysis.
- Looking for business rules within the report. For example, the sum, average, and percentage of specific fields may be created over and over and over again within the report. This could be a place where a more efficient design based on the business rule would be required.
- Profiling the data is more difficult because the business rules are calculated within the report layout. So we need to understand what makes up those calculations in the reports and write the quality checks.

Who thought this would be easy?

Idea 28: First Cuts at Compliance
David Loshin

Regulatory compliance is an interesting challenge for a couple of reasons. First, the imposition of new governmental regulations to which companies must adhere seems to be, to some degree, unfair, mostly because the government is essentially insisting that a company allocate funds toward observing the regulations with limited return on that investment (other than, perhaps, increased goodwill for not being noncompliant, if you know what I mean). Second, the creation of new regulations to which companies must adhere is an imposition on the agencies that are supposed to oversee that compliance. It means that they must spend their budget in ensuring that the companies remain complaint and to determine when companies are not compliant and to do something about that noncompliance.

> The perception, then, is that it is in everyone's best interest for the company to provide some kind of report and for the agency to focus on those companies that did not report.

Consider the whole situation from a practical (that is, budgetary) standpoint. For the company, the managers would like to limit expenditures on non-revenue-generating activity, so the objective is to spend the smallest amount of resources to appear to be as compliant as possible. For the government agency, which is probably already stretched thin with a limited budget and is being asked to monitor compliance with no increase in funding, the objective is to identify noncompliance when it appears to pose the greatest risk to citizens.

Let's apply this concept to regulatory reporting. Congress passes a law stating that companies must submit reports listing some sets of transactions to be compliant. The associated agency can fine companies that do not accurately report those transactions. Where do we start?

From the company's standpoint, not reporting would be a red flag, because it would then be implicitly noncompliant. From the agency's standpoint, allocating staff to review all transactions from all companies that report would require a significant resource investment; it's best to start with those companies that have not reported, because they are implicitly noncompliant. The perception, then, is that it is in everyone's best interest for the company to provide some kind of report and for the agency to focus on those companies that did not report.

So what about the question of the quality of that reported data? If this thought experiment is accurate, it will be up to a third party (such as an independent advisory or oversight watchdog, or investigative reporters) to identify data errors or inconsistencies.

Idea 29: Data Quality in Five Verbs
Jim Harris

Recently on Twitter, David Loshin asked the Twitterverse to propose the five most critical topics to communicate to data quality practitioners. My pithy response was that I propose five critical verbs: investigate, communicate, collaborate, remediate, and inebriate.

INVESTIGATE

Data quality is not exactly a riddle wrapped in a mystery inside an enigma. However, understanding your data is essential to using it effectively and improving its quality. Therefore, the first thing you must do is investigate.

So grab your favorite (preferably highly caffeinated) beverage, get settled into your comfy chair, roll up your sleeves, and starting analyzing

> Keep in mind that communication is mostly about listening.

that data. Data profiling tools can be helpful with raw data analysis. However, data profiling is elementary, my dear reader.

For you to make sense of those data elements, you require business context. This means you must talk with data's best friends—its stewards, analysts, and SMEs.

COMMUNICATE

After you have completed your preliminary investigation, the next thing you must do is communicate your findings. Communication improves everyone's understanding of how data is being used, verifies relevancy to business processes, and prioritizes critical data issues.

Keep in mind that communication is mostly about listening. Also, be prepared to face data denial when data quality problems are discussed. Most often, this is a natural self-defense mechanism for data and process owners because nobody likes to feel blamed for causing or failing to fix the data quality problems.

These discussions are essential to evaluating the potential ROI of data quality improvements, defining data quality standards, and most importantly, providing a working definition of success.

COLLABORATE

After you have investigated and communicated, you must rally the team that will work together to improve the quality of your data. A cross-disciplinary team will be needed. Data quality is neither a business nor a technical issue—because it is both.

Therefore, you need the collaborative effort of business and technical folks. The business folks usually own the data and understand its meaning and daily use. The technical folks usually own the hardware and software comprising your technical architecture. Both sets of folks must realize they are all "one company folk" that must collaborate to be successful.

No, you don't need a folk singer, but you require an executive sponsor. The need for collaboration might be rather obvious. However, as one of my favorite folk singers taught me, sometimes the hardest thing to learn is the least complicated.

REMEDIATE

Resolving data quality issues requires a combination of data cleansing and defect prevention. Data cleansing is reactive, and its common (and deserved) criticism is that it essentially treats the symptoms without curing the disease.

Defect prevention is proactive, and through root cause analysis and process improvements, it essentially is the cure for the quality issues that ail your data. However, a data governance framework is necessary for defect prevention to be successful—as is patience and understanding, because data prevention mandates a strategic organizational transformation that doesn't happen overnight.

The unavoidable reality is that data cleansing can correct today's problems while defect prevention is busy building a better tomorrow for your organization.

Fundamentally, data quality requires a hybrid discipline that combines data cleansing and defect prevention into an enterprise-wide best practice.

INEBRIATE

I am not necessarily advocating the drinking kind of inebriation. Instead, think Emily Dickinson. ("Inebriate of air am I" is a line from a poem about happiness, which yes, also makes a good drinking song.)

My point is that you must not only celebrate your successes, but celebrate them quite publicly. Channel yet another poet (Walt Whitman), and sound your barbaric yawp over the cubicles of your company: "We just improved the quality of our data!"

Of course, you need to be more specific. You should state your success using words illustrating the business impact of your achievements, such as mitigated risks, reduced costs, or increased revenue. Those three are always guaranteed executive crowd pleasers.

Also remember that you are not celebrating the end of your efforts; your data quality journey has only just begun. Avoid the peril of pursuing perfection, because you will never achieve it. However, with continued dedication, the quality of your data will get (returning to words from my favorite folk singers) "closer to fine."

Idea 30: Can Better-Quality Data Help Reduce Costs?
Joyce Norris-Montanari

You can use data quality management to analyze operational processes and the data manipulated in the processes to find inefficiencies. You can then correct these inefficiencies, thus leading to increased margins and profits. For the project I'm working on now, there are so many processes that seem redundant or nonessential that just the analysis of these processes would be beneficial. So, this is what we are going to do:

- Of those processes that we can affect, we are going to analyze and document each one.
- We will look for duplicate or redundant processes.
- We will profile to find duplicate or redundant data that is used in these processes.
- We will document all processes and data stores and profile across data stores looking for relationships.

- We will evaluate all the information gathered and identify processes that are suspect or possible processes for elimination.
- In our development and test environments, we will eliminate those processes and en-

> You can use data quality management to analyze operational processes and the data manipulated in the processes to find inefficiencies.

hance existing processes to make sure all business rules are still functioning prior to making changes to the production environment.

Of course, we won't forget to follow all change control procedures. Nor will we forget to make sure the business owners are involved and participating in this great cost savings exercise.

Idea 31: The Quality Gap: Why Being On-Time Isn't Enough
Jill Dyché

The biggest problem in business today is that everything is date driven and not quality driven.

There, I've said it. And a few dozen of my past and current clients are now sidling up to their laptops to shoot me an email asking me if this Idea is about them. (The answer: Yes it is, and you know who you are.) Seriously, this is a problem everywhere, yet despite the wholesale crises it precipitates, it's actually getting worse. The root cause of this problem is the old bugaboo of perception. "Progress" is usually measured by speed of delivery, not fitness for purpose, conformance to requirements, streamlined processes, or any of those other quality maxims. We've all heard a variation of the following:

Just [complete the work] so I can get it into my status report for this [week/month/year].

So that project manager's boss is now satisfied that the team is getting things done instead of abusing flex time or work-from-home policies. In the meantime, the campaign went to a saturated segment. Product prices no longer match across divisions. Account managers are confused about territory assignments and are cannibalizing sales. And the Feds have just left a message for your chief financial officer (CFO).

You have to name it to claim it. (I learned this from watching *The Biggest Loser* the other night.) So herewith, the five main reasons for this phenomenon:

1. **The measurement conversation, which isn't baked into project initiation:** In our business intelligence (BI), MDM, and data governance projects, we make sure that this is part of the requirements

> The biggest problem in business today is that everything is date driven and not quality driven.

phase. But practitioners aren't the only people who need to have this conversation. Business executives and managers should be proactive about their quality criteria during ideation or (at the latest) in the business case. This not only elucidates delivery steps, it makes scoping so much easier.

2. **The "effort delusion," that anachronistic WASP-y assumption that many people working hard will yield positive results:** There's a monkeys-on-an-island analogy here that I'll refrain from making. But as many before me have aptly observed, working hard simply isn't enough.

3. **The open loop:** Imagine how many companies have invested in quality programs, data quality automation, business analysis skills, TQM and SixSigma training, and other improvements yet continue to fail to reconcile the project's original objectives from its delivered outcome. Instead, projects endure scope creep or are delivered as a shadow of their original vision. Closing the loop between original vision and ultimate deliverable is a learned and practiced behavior. Instead, mediocre projects drive a flurry of fix-and-maintain activities that would have been unnecessary had they been delivered right the first time, and ultimately far more costly.

4. **Failure to define realistic delivery increments:** This is Project Management 101. Or is it? The problem here is that the people

doing the scoping are often not those on the hook to deliver the goods. I've seen project managers idling in the doorways asking programmers to rattle off their tasks, then randomly assigning time to completion. It doesn't work that way. Or it shouldn't.

5. **The economic climate that has made people paranoid:** There, I've said it. And a few dozen of my past and current clients…oh, never mind. You've seen it yourself. People go into delivery hyperdrive and start producing at all costs. ("Just load the data into the database—we'll worry about whether it's usable later.") Worse, they cover their collective asses while spinning stories of their productivity, backing into post-facto project plans and pointing fingers when people ask questions.

Maybe if we understand the root causes, we can fix the problem. (Thanks for that one too, Bob and Jillian!) Or maybe we'll just stay on the couch and keep chomping away, occasionally groping for the remote control so we can get something different just by pressing a button.

Idea 32: Data Quality Improvement—Don't Forget the Basics
Dylan Jones

If you are serious about improving data quality, don't forget some of those simple techniques that can really help you leverage investments in technology and people.

Here are some common mistakes that I typically find, even in mature organizations with fully fledged data quality initiatives.

LACK OF SYSTEM DOCUMENTATION STANDARDS

If I walked into your company and asked for the latest design specification for your customer billing system, would you be able to provide it quickly? Would it be accurate and accessible, trusted and relevant?

In my experience, the answer is typically, "No" or "Go speak to Jane in support; she's been here since the 80s."

This lack of documentation means that you have no insight into how complex business logic was originally coded. Without this information, you have to rely solely on anecdotal evidence and re-engineering, which are time consuming and seldom give the complete picture.

LACK OF DATA MODELING BEST PRACTICES

Having an early background in software development, I know that many product development teams pay lip service to data modeling best practices. Data models are meant to be a key enabler of application design but, in reality, they are often perceived as an administrative chore. In many cases, they are either out of date or were simply never created in the first place.

Take a look at your data modeling standards. Are changes in table structure and relationships reflected in an updated physical and logical model? Is there a conceptual model available? How does that relate to the enterprise schema? Do you have an enterprise schema?

Accurate data models are critical to understanding how to construct your library of data quality rules.

LACK OF BUSINESS RULES DOCUMENTATION

Managing data quality effectively requires a deep understanding of how your company delivers its services.

To some extent, you can re-engineer simple data and business rules, but it's laborious and error prone. The core business rules that drive customer value (and profits) need to be documented for you to create data quality rules to monitor them and eliminate defects in the service chain.

Can you produce an accurate and accessible source of all the business rules that are in effect across your key business services? Does this include that little tweak the users have adopted because the new system won't allow the old product codes?

A lot of business rules documentation comes in the form of disparate instructions in out-of-date manuals locked away in straining bookcases. Improving data quality demands knowledge of how your business delivers services in the real world, warts and all.

LACK OF USER FEEDBACK FACILITIES

Data quality management requires outside-in and inside-out approaches. Tools can help you gather insight from inside systems using profiling and discovery functionality, but you also need to mine user anecdotes and experiences from the outside.

Are you making some quick-wins by listening to the workforce and your customers? Do you have a feedback and complaints system that is available for mining and intelligence gathering? What do your users think about the quality of the data they

> Improving data quality demands knowledge of how your business delivers services in the real world, warts and all.

handle or create? Do they like the new systems that have been introduced? Are trends or performance indicators available?

Focusing solely on an inside-out data quality approach will deliver issues without context. Listen to workers and customers to help you focus and align technology efforts.

LACK OF VERSION CONTROL AND AUDITING

If you observe a large spike or dip in daily data quality levels in your service fulfillment system, can you instantly see whether any code fixes, data feeds, application upgrades, or other system changes were carried out?

When was that last table amended? Who made the change? Why was it made? Who signed off on it?

Why invest in data quality monitoring software without understanding the external factors that can lead to those defects?

You need to take a holistic approach when managing data quality, and that starts with documenting all the environmental factors that impact your data.

LACK OF INFORMATION CHAIN MANAGEMENT

Do you know the precise lineage of the data items in your business area? Can you trace all the intricate data flows and transformations of your financial data before it arrives in your annual report? Do you know who is responsible for maintaining this information along the chain? Do you have service-level agreements (SLAs) set up with data suppliers from different departments or organizations? Who is responsible for the data feed processes that link the different systems/business units? Are these feed processes audited and version controlled?

Knowing the life story and path of the data you use to make decisions, deliver services, and drive profits is vital.

Technology can help, but information chains, by their very nature, are never static. They need to be accurately documented and well governed to sustain long-term data quality improvement.

IN SUMMARY

These are just six basic practices I often see lacking in organizations embarking on data quality initiatives. There are many more.

The lesson is an obvious one. If you want to get the most out of your data quality investment in people and tools, make sure you are also delivering on the basics.

Anything else is false economy.

Idea 33: Assessing the Enterprise

Joyce Norris-Montanari

Good luck getting an entire enterprise's data needs and usage assessed in the near future. Isn't that always the issue? The data—it's always about the data!

If you are one of the companies that has not created an enterprise inventory, then continue reading this idea. You have to understand the data and computer systems for the corporation, but how can you do that quickly? My suggestions follow:

- Create the inventory of systems and data as you are embarking upon new corporate initiatives.
- Document the system, the platform, and all the data components (database, tables, fields).
- Rely on data models with definitions where possible.
- Use any data profiling tools that you have to help get the documentation to really identify this information.

> The data—it's always about the data!

- Interview and question management and IT staff members to determine any other needs. Ask questions like these:
  o What systems do you use?
  o Does that system meet your needs?
  o Is there other information that you require to do your job?
- Coordinate and centralize data management efforts.
- Use change control meetings to help understand the corporate data requirements.
- Centralize the sharing of this information for the corporation. I like to use SharePoint if my customer has it; otherwise, I look toward internal websites.

Idea 34: Playing the Hand You're Dealt: Data Quality and SLAs
Jill Dyché

One of the biggest challenges in implementing a true data quality strategy across business and IT is articulating the goal. Sure, clean data is the desired outcome, and data usability is key. But it's not realistic to expect IT to know how business users across departments, subsidiaries, and geographies define data quality or to understand the acceptance metrics for "good data."

Data quality includes ensuring that the data represents the data definitions and rules established by the business. Data should reflect the values that exist in the operational systems. The challenge is when operational systems have errors or business rules conflict with the actual source data.

This challenge is compounded by the realization that "perfect data" requires more effort than "imperfect data." There's a balancing act between delivering high-quality, clean, complete data and delivering that data quickly to the businesses that need it. The idea behind an SLA is that IT won't have to guess what that balance is; it can establish the balance from the outset. The business should be responsible for articulating how clean it wants the data versus how quickly it wants the data. It needs to establish the trade-offs between manpower and data availability.

So consider the balancing act that many IT organizations are forced to endure when it comes to data quality. On the one hand, the business demands perfect data. One could argue there's no such thing as perfect data, but it's still a lofty goal. On the other hand, the business

> There's a balancing act between delivering high-quality, clean, complete data and delivering that data quickly to the businesses that need it.

wants its data delivered quickly. Each goal makes the other one that much harder to achieve.

We recently witnessed a real-life version of this quandary. As part of its overall CRM strategy, one of our large casino clients encourages new players to sign up for loyalty cards. A player can apply for the loyalty card on the spot. The goal of the casino floor staff is to expedite the application process and get the player back to the craps table or the roulette wheel as soon as possible.

However, the casino's marketing organization has a different set of goals. It would like the player's address to be standardized to support future direct marketing and reduce returned mail costs. It's implied real-time address cleansing and standardization.

The SLA established that address cleansing could not force the customer to wait for more than 60 seconds. It turned out that marketing people were comfortable waiting several days for that player's address to be cleansed and standardized, as long as they had access to accurate customer data by the time they were ready to do the first follow-up mailing. Had the business analysts in the IT organization focused on the casino operations group, the SLA would have mandated a potentially costly real-time solution.

But by engaging stakeholders across business functions and establishing a realistic SLA, IT realized it could implement address cleansing in batch, not real-time, thereby saving considerable budget money while keeping varied business constituents happy.

Now that's service!

Idea 35: Building for the Future
Dylan Jones

Most organizations I encounter focus on tactical data quality initiatives. These are typically time-boxed projects that are bit-part players in a broader strategic play.

For example, there may be a data quality improvement project to ensure data is fit for a complex data migration. Perhaps there is an M&A in progress and data assets need to be consolidated to truly deliver on the strategic value offered by joining two businesses. Although the merger is strategic, the data quality element can at best be described as tactical.

I do occasionally come across some organizations that put in place more strategic, long-term data quality improvements. In one example, a process monitoring and root-cause alerting initiative regularly saves the company millions of dollars per year by eliminating data defects before they can inflict financial damage. In so many of those situations, however, there's a common theme: the techniques are not being shared, so the gains are lost on a corporate level.

If we take a data migration project as an example, there are so many gains that can be retained, built upon, and shared with the wider enterprise. Many of these are covered frequently in the Ideas in this book.

In my root-cause prevention example, this is a fantastic case of a highly innovative approach that is

> If you're responsible for data quality in your organization, there are some simple techniques you can use to slowly extend the reach of your data quality capability.

generating real value to the business. You would expect other parts of the business that have the same type of processes to adopt a similar solution, wouldn't you? Sadly, no. I haven't seen this adopted anywhere else in the organization.

For a variety of reasons, many organizations create value through data quality or other data-driven initiatives. However, that value is far too often lost when that project terminates. Consider the following questions:

- Is this happening in your business?
- At the end of every data-driven project, what happens to all the analysis and research undertaken?
- Is the data stored on a Wiki or shared resource for future projects?

If you're responsible for data quality in your organization, there are some simple techniques you can use to slowly extend the reach of your data quality capability. It's wise to create a simple exit interview with the project leader of each data-driven project.

When such a project ends, the questions change. Here are some new questions to consider:

- Who are the *new* data stakeholders resulting from the project?
- What are the implications of data defects in the systems and services that now depend on the project?
- Which staff members were involved in data analysis or data quality activities?
- What skills or tools did staff members utilize?
- Who was the prime sponsor for the project, and what were the criteria for success both post-project and ongoing?
- Is it likely that reduced data quality will influence the sponsor's vision of success?

Beyond this, I'd look to see what information can be retained and stored in a central repository. (Think Wiki or SharePoint folder—something electronic, accessible, and visible. Printed documentation in a filing cabinet is of limited value.)

- Can you perform a simple data quality impact survey of the systems and services resulting from the project? This is good governance because it represents a proactive approach, identifying hotspots that can be far more costly to resolve down the line.
- Can you interview some of the other project members, lead developers, business analysts, and data architects? These folks often squirrel vital information that needs to be shared and recorded. They'll also give you a far more detailed picture of where the data quality issues are likely to arise.
- If interim data quality processes and techniques were adopted, can you document and share them with the wider company?

For instance, I recently consulted with an organization that openly admitted to having multiple customer consolidation projects working independently. The opportunity for knowledge sharing in modern businesses is phenomenal, and it's largely untapped.

Putting a sales and marketing hat on, I'd build a standard report of your findings, the long-term data quality needs, the knowledge gained, and how to use this to further enterprise data quality aspirations. If you have a regular newsletter to senior management and the wider data quality community in your business, circulate your findings, directing traffic to any resources you have stored away.

But why bother with all this? I can see some obvious benefits:

- The costs are actually minimal; much of the process can be semi-automated, but overall this simple activity will directly help the company save time and money.
- If you're responsible for data quality, you can't wait for projects to come to you. You need to create a noninvasive, proactive method of understanding where your company is driving its data forward and how you can support its wider strategic goals.
- You will increasingly be viewed as an asset—something that adds value, as opposed to a cost center—which is sensible in this economic climate.
- There are pockets of data quality skill in your business that are often lost or remain hidden. This process can help uncover them so you can save the hassle and expense of hiring external resources.

In summary, organizations need to start holding on to some of the knowledge, tools, and experience that reside in our companies and begin the process of building longer-term data quality initiatives.

Is your organization taking a structured approach to lock in the knowledge gained on current data-driven projects? Are you doing anything constructive to further data quality progress in your business? Do you have anything to add to the previous points?

Idea 36: The SME Shadow Knows
Jim Harris

Although the original radio drama *The Shadow* was before my time, my grandparents often quoted its famous tagline ("Who knows what evil lurks in the hearts of men? The Shadow knows!") and the maniacal laughter that traditionally followed it. The Shadow was a crime-fighting vigilante with psychic powers.

As a mild-mannered consultant doing battle with the dark forces of poor data quality, psychic powers would definitely be helpful in discovering those undocumented business rules that are the bane of a successful data quality program.

This tacit knowledge (see Idea 9, which discusses Eternal September) is often trapped within the minds of the organization's many data stewards, business analysts, and SMEs.

> Part of the challenge is that, because SMEs are experts, they can't imagine what it's like not to know what they know.

Although it might be cathartic to think of this knowledge as the evil that lurks in their diabolical job security plans, the truth is that many SMEs find it challenging to formalize what they know into a document or other means that can be easily shared with, and understood by, others lacking their extensive experience.

THE CURSE OF KNOWLEDGE
The real super-villain is the Curse of Knowledge, which the Heath brothers explain in their great book *Made to Stick: Why Some Ideas Survive and Others Die.*

> *Once you know something, it's hard to imagine not knowing it. And that, in turn, makes it harder for you to communicate clearly to a novice.*

Part of the challenge is that, because SMEs are experts, they can't imagine what it's like not to know what they know. They struggle to explain their knowledge because "you can't unlearn what you already know."

In addition, the pearls of wisdom you are searching for are often just a small fraction of the vast tacit knowledge that the SMEs possess.

THE SME SHADOW

The most effective approach I have found for overcoming the challenge of the Curse of Knowledge is to become the crime-fighting vigilante with psychic powers known only as the SME Shadow.

Unfortunately, it's not as cool as it sounds. In fact, it's likely to sound creepy to the SMEs, because you basically sit in their cubicle with them and watch them work. Occasionally you might get up the courage to ask them what are, understandably from their perspective, stupid questions.

In physics, the observer effect[3] refers to changes that the act of observation makes on what is being observed. And in psychology, the observer-expectancy effect refers to how people may change their behavior when they're aware of being watched. Both of these effects can lead to ineffective knowledge transfer, despite the best of intentions from both the SME and the SME Shadow.

However, sometimes the only way to learn what the SMEs already know is to observe them applying their knowledge during their daily activities. So queue the dramatic music because what I am trying to say is this: who knows what undocumented business rules lurk in the minds of SMEs? The SME Shadow knows!

Idea 37: The Myth of the "Golden Record"
David Loshin

There is a general perception that by installing and populating an MDM tool, the organization immediately benefits from the consolidation of multiple representations of data into a single "golden record." Also referred to as a "single source of truth," this concept suggests that a byproduct of data consolidation is the materialization of one representation whose quality and correctness exceed that of any other representation for any application purpose.

---

3. http://en.wikipedia.org/wiki/Observer_effect_(physics)

Relying on the creation of a golden record may not necessarily provide the value expected for a number of reasons, including these:

- The semantics associated with a master data concept may differ among the application uses, which may lead to confusion (at the least) and incorrect operation (at the worst).
- The survivorship rules may cleanse out pieces of information that may be irrelevant in most contexts but critical in a limited number of situations.
- There is a need for clearly determining which attributes are to be incorporated into a single golden record; consequently, there may be confusion in choosing between locally managed data attributes and master data attributes.

In addition, the rules associated with managing that golden record need to accommodate the union of all the rules associated with managing the original replicas that are consolidated into that master version, as well as managing the data quality expectations associated with all downstream consumers. Not only is this an engineering challenge, it may expose situations in which those business rules conflict with each other.

> Relying on the creation of a golden record may not necessarily provide the value expected.

It is more reasonable to consider the use of a master record in two other scenarios: either as a method for accumulating and presenting the collected sets of data associated with a recognized entity, or as a data quality method for identity resolution and differentiation of entities.

Idea 38: When a Date Goes Wrong
Joyce Norris-Montanari

The date data type options are unique to each database management system (SQLServer, Oracle, Sybase, DB2, Teradata, MySQL). Some date options include representing the first day of January of this year in the following ways:

- Jan-01-12
- 01-01-2012
- January 1, 2012
- 01/01/2012 or 01/01/12

Adding the element of time to the date to create a date/timestamp creates additional variations. You can also include date:hh:mm:ss, where hour of the day, minutes, and seconds are added to the date data type. Although this option does allow you to create something unique in a row of data, you can still get duplicates in a second's time. So, some database management systems add on a sequence number at the end of the time portion of the date/timestamp. This ensures uniqueness, especially if concatenated with another field in the table to create a composite primary key.

> Some database management systems add a sequence number at the end of the time portion of the date/timestamp.

When profiling a field that should be a date but is in the database as a character or a variable character (varchar) field, you may want to consider the following:

- If it is a free-form field with no consistency in the date format, the data quality or ETL process needs to translate what is in the field to a consistent date format for uniform query.
- After analyzing that data and validating that the field does contain dates, use the profiler function for frequency and pattern analysis to decipher exactly how to set up those programs and handle all the different date formats.
- It might be good to change the source system based on the profiled data.

It's no wonder dates are always an issue!

Idea 39: Does This Data Model Make Me Look Fat?
Jill Dyché

I used to attend a certain conference popular with data modelers. Data modelers are a peculiar breed. They all know one another. They stop each other in the hallways between workshops, arguing over modeling conventions, debating semantic layers, and commiserating over user availability. During coffee breaks you can read the bubbles above their heads that say, "My management doesn't really understand what I do."

I know this because I myself was once a data modeler. I kept various iterations of an entity relationship (E/R) diagram on my office wall. I could argue Kimball or Inmon with equal ease. I used the word "tuple" in mixed company. Known for lobbying executives to attend model walkthrough sessions—yet never too confident to forget the requisite haul of baked goods—I once tried explaining the transgression of a "dangling foreign key" to a

> The same skills that have been classically applied to developing and maintaining a data model can in fact accelerate nascent governance efforts by translating business requirements into data requirements, deploying new business rules and policies, leveraging incumbent metadata, and formalizing data stewardship.

CFO who had innocently asked about customer-account linkage. My bad.

Then one night, two masked men threw me in the back of a van and forced me to drink an opaque elixir. The next thing I remember, I was waking up screaming, "Just give me my friggin report already!" with an incinerated copy of Ted Codd's 12 Rules still smoldering under my bed.

That was years ago. I'm now starting to come around again to thinking that data modeling is important. Before you back up the Econoline, let me explain that though I do believe that modeling data itself is important, it's the message around the data model that gets us into trouble. As much mastery as we've achieved around our data models and subsequent database designs, our attempts to convince business colleagues to appreciate our work are still met with eye-rolling and impatient sighs.

Our fanatical emphasis on the data model belies the more important point: we have cultivated a set of disciplines to design information that enables business needs.

Nowadays I recommend data modeling as the foundation for broader and more visible data governance efforts. The same skills that have been classically applied to developing and maintaining a data model can in fact accelerate nascent governance efforts by translating business requirements into data requirements, deploying new business rules and policies, leveraging incumbent metadata, and formalizing data stewardship.

Indeed, show me a data modeler intimate with his company's data requirements and sources, and I'll show you the newest member of the Data Governance Council. With our clients, we've discovered that the existence of a robust data model is a positive indicator of the company's data governance readiness.

In my dilettante data modeling days, I learned a lot about data relationships, structures, and usage. My colleagues and I applied that knowledge to broader business initiatives. We made sure that data had a seat at the table with every new business program.

So, my data modeler brothers and sisters: you may have new career "dimensions" to explore. What? You're good, you say? Okay. I'm in your driveway right now in a big white van. Get in. Now drink this.

Idea 40: Relationships Trump Data, For Now
Rich Murnane

I've seen this now a couple times over the past few years, and it's definitely something I wouldn't have understood a few years ago: relationships trump nearly everything in business, especially data.

Many contracts for services include clauses requiring data about performance on the contract to be submitted to the client on a regular basis. Many people naively believe that if the service provider does not deliver on this contracted item, the entire contract will be lost and the client will look for a new service provider. I can tell you this is not what I'm seeing from the front lines of the data management war. What I'm seeing is service providers making various levels of effort to provide the data in the required format at schedules they can meet. I can also tell you I'm really not seeing any of these service providers meeting all the requirements, such as these:

- Following the prescribed format of data (for example, providing a fixed-width text file in which characters 1–9 represent one field (name), characters 12–30 represent another (address), etc.

- Delivering the data on time
- Delivering all the data; either fields are left null, they're filled with default values, or the records are just plain missing
- Delivering accurate data, again, both depth (all the records) and breath (all the fields are correct)
- Delivering the data via the correct channel (FTP, Secure FTP, Managed File Transfer, email, and so on)

You would think that large service providers wouldn't sign up for service contracts if they could not meet one or more of the requirements of the contract. This is what I thought for years. You would also think that if all the requirements of the contract are not met, the client would run and cancel the contract and look for a new service provider. The reality is, however, these larger service contracts consist of a multitude of requirements. If the service provider is meeting the one or two primary objectives of the contract very well and it has built a good relationship with the client, it is unlikely to lose the contract if it doesn't meet some of the "less important" requirements. And unfortunately for us data geeks out there, "data" typically falls into this "less important" bucket.

> Requirements for data in large service contracts will become important enough that if service providers are not meeting their obligations, it will begin to sour their relationships with their clients.

Now, I'm not advocating that all you service providers start ignoring the data requirements in these large contracts, but I am going to give you a little hint into what is about to come your way. Data is becoming more and more important to everyone, and requirements for data in large service contracts will become important enough that if service providers are not meeting their obligations, it will begin to sour their relationships with their clients.

An example: Let's say your shop provides school bus services to the local public schools in your county. Along comes the public school system from the next county looking for school bus services. (I'm just making this up, by the way.) Congratulations! You win the contract. Note, however, that embedded on page 23 of the contract you just won is a paragraph or two requiring you to provide metrics each month back to the new client. You'll need to email a comma-separated value (CSV) document containing certain fields (columns) of data via Secure FTP, once a month. Instead of complying with this contractual item, you think that you should be okay if you just email the client a Microsoft Excel document containing the fields of data you have about this client's bus trips. This may suffice if you provide bus drivers dressed up as superheroes and Disney princesses, but sooner or later that client is going to become tech-savvy enough that the data you are supposed to be providing becomes more important to the client, and it is going to forget about your costume-wearing bus drivers and look elsewhere for a better bus service.

In summary, data is becoming more and more important. Even though, in today's world, "relationships trump data" in most businesses, sooner or later, "data will drive relationships"—and not meeting contractual data requirements will be seriously frowned upon.

Idea 41: Accuracy Is Not an Annual Event
Dylan Jones

A family friend of ours works for a charity. The charity is beginning to look at its campaign to attract donors for 2011/2012, and it noticed that a fairly large percentage of calendars sent out at Christmas to past donors had been returned.

The reason, of course, came down to accuracy. People move, get divorced, pass away, or simply fill in the wrong details on a regular basis.

All of this meant that the charity had been witnessing a steady degradation of its most vital asset

> Trying to inject accuracy in 12-month spikes is like trying to recalibrate the equipment in a manufacturing plant once a year.

over time: donor contact details. Of course, if charities are using email as their primary contact route with donors, the degradation can be even worse.

To remedy this, the charity is considering an annual data cleansing "heave-ho" to help clean up its data.

The problem with this approach is that trying to inject accuracy in 12-month spikes is like trying to recalibrate the equipment in a manufacturing plant once a year. Cars will come off the line in perfect condition the first week, but by the end of the year you'll be churning out faulty cars day after day until the next "fix" comes along.

The same issue applies to service processes that depend on high-quality data.

As personal contact details change throughout the year but are not reflected in the data, accuracy creeps away, leaving wasted opportunities as marketing efforts fail to hit the mark.

How should the charity resolve this?

The answer isn't to cleanse the data using spikes of improvement. Instead, the charity needs simpler accuracy touch-points with donors. Make it easier for the charity to gather contact detail changes and for donors to inform them of changes. Here are some ideas:

- Give donors a way to notify the charity via social media pathway.
- Have a prominent email or contact telephone number on existing contact material so donors can update their details easily. (The charity had no visible process for doing this.)
- Text donors if mail is returned.
- Carry out address verification/cleansing on a real-time basis so the charity doesn't have to wait 12 months to verify donor data.

Although cost is a challenge here, what is the cost of one donor not contributing for the coming year or a business failing to be notified of your new sponsorship package?

Figures like this can be calculated crudely by looking at average contribution per donor segment, examining how much post is returned by segment, and working out the ROI of improvements.

The reality is that data accuracy is not a one-time event. It's a perpetual function, but so many companies I've worked with in the past treat it as a spring cleaning exercise before a big campaign.

You have to build opportunities for accuracy improvement into multiple touch-points with whatever asset you want to manage: customers, equipment, products, services, contracts, and so on.

Idea 42: Knowing Your Customers, in Spite of Your Industry
Jill Dyché

Mark, one of our managing consultants, recently remarked that our vertical industry skills were no longer as important to our clients as they used to be.

I found this hard to swallow. After all, our consultants' industry knowledge allows us to speak our clients' language, and most of our consultants have deep expertise in at least one vertical. Mark maintained that retail industry expertise was paramount, because deep down every company is really in the retail business.

Ultimately, Mark was driving at a larger issue. He thinks that industry skills are a Trojan horse for something more important. What he really means is that the ability to help companies leverage information to understand and monitor customer preferences and behaviors is broader than any single industry. And weeding out professionals who understand how to deliver these diverse capabilities is far more challenging than finding someone who shares the same industry vocabulary.

> Even more critical are the skills to recognize who the customer is—across sales channels, territories, product sets, and siloed systems—and how he or she interacts with the company over time.

Customer purchase trends, actions, and requests—and how all these affect top and bottom line growth—involve deep, entrenched skill sets that hinge on intimacy with consumerism. Finding, reconciling, standardizing, integrating, and deploying information about how customers buy, interact, request support, and expect us to communicate in a relevant way is a complex specialty. All companies, regardless of vertical industry, market segment, or size, need to analyze customer interactions so they can manage and improve their customer relationships and drive profits.

As we spend more time with companies, we discover that their real challenge is knowing—not guessing—who their customers are and what they do. Of course, insight into individual products and services is still important. But even more critical are the skills to recognize who the customer is—across sales channels, territories, product sets, and siloed systems—and how he or she interacts with the company over time.

This is as significant for our clients' business customers as it is for their individual consumers—perhaps even more so when a few large businesses can claim a percentage point or two of the company's overall revenue. Business customers are different because of their purchase volumes, pricing levels, and product usage, but fundamentally businesses are still made up of individuals. So understanding how people need to be supported, sold to, and interacted with remains a lofty and ultimately transcendent objective for most companies, regardless of the products they sell.

Idea 43: Defending the Data
Phil Simon

For better or (mostly) worse, in my professional career, I have consistently found myself on projects suffering from a bevy of issues, many of which were related to data. By 2008, I had reached a tipping point: I was either going to write a book about IT project failures or see a shrink. I chose the former.

In other words, it's rare that, as a consultant, I have the power to influence the direction of an organization's data management practices. I find myself these days in such a place. The details of my project aren't particularly interesting to the average reader. For now, however, suffice it to say that I am building a little ETL tool that takes a bunch of data from a bunch of places, transforms it, and spits it out to a bunch of people. I'd give this

> Although I'm a big fan of Agile development, constantly changing things is hardly efficient.

about a 4 on my 1–10 scale for complexity. (Yes, I have had to build tools that scored a 14 on that same 1–10 scale before. Take me out for a beer sometime, and I'll tell you a story or two.)

On my current assignment, I'm working with a large financial institution in the midst of some M&A activity. I'm working closely with a director named Dave. (That's not his real name; I just happen to be listening to the Foo Fighters right now, and their front man is ridiculously talented Dave Grohl.) Director Dave is getting pulled in many directions and, using more tact than I have, is trying to successfully navigate his organization's political waters. As soon as we make the changes to file formats for his internal clients, he almost just as quickly comes back with changes and "the new final" formats.

Although I'm a big fan of Agile development, constantly changing things is hardly efficient. The other day, Dave told me that we just had to make three changes to "descriptions" that should be quite easy. I furrowed my brow, telling Dave that things weren't quite as simple as that. His "descriptions" were my fields on multiple tables and queries. Without going into a lot of detail, the changes involved a decent amount of work.

But then something strange happened: Dave watched me make these changes for an hour. I'd run the Access-based ETL tool and shown him how these ostensibly minor changes caused the whole thing to break. We had developed this on the fly because (spoiler coming) the whole tool was due well before I started.

Armed with a newfound appreciation of the major impact of minor changes, Dave vowed to do two things:

- Run any changes by me before agreeing to make them, even if they seem insignificant.
- Immediately say no to changes that appear to be major.

Through this agreement, Dave was minimizing the chance that excessive changes would break the ETL tool and compromise what he was sending out. In short, Dave was defending the data.

SIMON SAYS

My life would be a great deal easier if more clients stuck up for their data. In my experience, most people just want what they want when they want it. They don't understand concepts such as data integrity, referential integrity, master data, and the like. One could argue that not everyone needs to know what we data management professionals know. Perhaps that's true. But an appreciation for the data goes a long way toward ensuring that things don't completely spiral out of control.

Idea 44: Oughtn't You Audit?
Jim Harris

Ensuring that the data being used to make critical business decisions is as reliable and accurate as possible is why data quality is so vitally important to the success of your organization. That statement would probably make most people throughout your organization nod their head in an ostentatious demonstration of agreement with this universally acknowledged truth.

So why then do these same people never do the following:

- Check that data is complete and accurate before sharing it with others
- Seek to understand what the data means within a business context
- Consider the costs and other risks associated with poor data quality
- Verify the data they are using to make critical business decisions

CLAP YOUR HANDS IF YOU BELIEVE IN DATA QUALITY

Many organizations treat data quality like Tinker Bell and the other fairies in *Peter Pan*, who only exist as long as children believe in them. In the theatrical production, Tinker Bell is portrayed on stage using a tiny flashing light. At the end of Act Two when she is dying, Peter Pan asks the children in the audience to clap their hands if they believe in fairies. The louder the children clap, the brighter the light (Tinker Bell) shines. When the audience claps at the end of one of my data quality presentations, I simply can't help but wonder: do they really believe in data quality?

> Many organizations treat data quality like Tinker Bell and the other fairies in *Peter Pan*, who only exist as long as children believe in them.

AUDIT AUGHT OR AUDIT NAUGHT?

Often it seems that organizations have an aught or naught (all or nothing) approach to data quality often revealed by their data auditing practices.

Instead of "If it ain't broke, don't fix it," audit-naughters use their data on a daily basis following the mantra, "If we don't check to see if it's broken, we won't have to fix it." That's in opposition to audit-aughters, who become trapped in analysis paralysis and delay or prevent critical business decisions because of "grave concerns about the data."

These two views resemble the Pair of Perilous Ps (Procrastination and Perfection) that I previously wrote about in my blog posting "Data Quality and the Middle Way."

KNOWING IS HALF THE BATTLE

While audit-aughters believe knowledge of poor quality requires resolving every data issue before acting upon it, audit-naughters prefer to believe "ignorance is bliss." However, by performing an audit, you will simply know how good or poor the quality of your data really is. And as Jackson Beck taught us: "Knowing is half the battle."

Of course, the other half of the battle is formulating a realistic plan to continuously monitor as well as incrementally improve the quality of your data. Without performing an audit, for aught you know, all is well with the data you've got, and perhaps naught is wrong at all—but then again, perhaps it is.

Therefore, if your organization really believes in the vital importance of data quality, oughtn't you audit?

Idea 45: Groundhog Data Quality Day
Jim Harris

Sometimes, when you're suffering from poor data quality, it can feel like you're having the worst data management day—over and over again.

Every year in the United States and Canada, folks celebrate Groundhog Day. According to a scientifically proven fact (okay, folklore), if a groundhog sees its shadow when it emerges from its burrow, winter will continue for six more weeks. In the movie *Groundhog Day*, Bill Murray stars as Phil Connors, a TV weatherman sent to Punxsutawney, Pennsylvania to report live from the scene where Punxsutawney Phil, the famous Master Marmot of Prognostication, would determine the remaining duration of the winter season. After a winter storm strands him in Punxsutawney, Phil Connors awakes on what he thinks is the next day only to discover that it's Groundhog Day all over again, and throughout the movie he relives that same day over and over again.

GROUNDHOG DATA QUALITY DAY

When the organization's only approach to data quality is reactive data cleansing projects, it can seem like it's data quality déjà vu all over again, aka Groundhog Data Quality Day.

Although I accept the reality that reactive data cleansing will always have a starring role in the data quality movie, proactive defect prevention should get top billing because whenever it's possible, processes should be improved to prevent the same defects from happening over and over again. Groundhog Data Quality Day happens most frequently at organizations that do not have a dedicated data quality team or data stewardship function. These organizations take a volunteer firefighting approach to data quality.

VOLUNTEER DATA FIREFIGHTERS

Volunteer data firefighters are a data cleansing project team temporarily brought together to address data quality issues when they get too big to ignore. After the project is over, volunteer data firefighters go back to their regular jobs, only to be once again called to action when the next inevitable poor data quality blaze starts burning.

Now, I admit that it's always more difficult for an organization to get funding for a proactive measure than a reactive one. For example, you don't need to convince executive management that putting out

> It's always more difficult for an organization to get funding for a proactive measure than a reactive one.

the blazing data fire that is burning down their business would be a really good idea. However, practicing fire (that is, defect) prevention is obviously important, and many fires could have been avoided or at least minimized if the organization had invested in building its systems "up to code"—such as by not constructing a data warehouse out of obviously flammable material. (No validation rules are enforced during data entry. Really?)

Of course, practicing fire prevention will not guarantee that a fire couldn't still happen, just like there is a difference between flame-resistant and nonflammable materials. Something in the building is capable of catching fire, and fires always find a way to spread. So do data quality problems.

IF THERE IS NO TOMORROW

If your organization only performs reactive data cleansing and keeps putting off practicing proactive defect prevention until tomorrow, you should consider the wise words of Phil Connors:

Well, what if there is no tomorrow? There wasn't one today!

Idea 46: When Data Quality Breaks Bad

Phil Simon

I recently became addicted (pun intended) to the AMC show *Breaking Bad*. It's about a 50-year old high school chemistry teacher who finds out that he has lung cancer. With a pregnant wife, a young son with cerebral palsy, and little in the way of money and time to live, he "breaks bad." That is, he begins manufacturing crystal meth.

Fascinating stuff, Phil, but this isn't a forum for your favorite TV shows.

Understood, but there was a point to my little intro. The show got me thinking about how and why data quality breaks bad in an organization. Is there a specific point at which data quality breaks bad? Allow me to posit four.

LOSS OF A KEY EMPLOYEE

We've all seen this before. Walt is the one person who knows how everything works. He's able to seamlessly navigate the sea of disparate systems, applications, databases, and interfaces and get to the root of an issue. He's also really proactive and fixes many problems before they become serious. Unfortunately, for one reason or another, he leaves. His replacement fails to hit the ground running.

SIMON SAYS: HOW TO PREVENT BREAKING BAD

Much like banks being too big to fail, some employees are too important to lose. Know who they are, try like hell to keep them happy so they'll stay, and make sure that you have backup in the event of an unanticipated departure.

UPGRADE OR PATCH

Your software vendor issues a patch to fix a known bug (er, "undocumented feature"). Or perhaps you have to upgrade to the vendor's latest version. In any event, your system and apps were working fine one day and then, all of a sudden, they're broken. If it's an egregious error, perhaps it will become obvious to end users running reports or looking at balances. If the problem is less obvious, however, it can be months or years before an issue is caught.

Simon Says: How to Prevent Breaking Bad

Carefully test any patches or upgrades. Tie out numbers. Don't be on the bleeding edge of an app (or new version) unless it is absolutely necessary.

TOO MUCH WORK/TOO FEW RESOURCES

The Great Recession has hit many organizations hard. Many people are swamped with work and have a hard time just getting through the day. They simply don't have enough time to do everything that they should do.

Simon Says: How to Prevent Breaking Bad

It's easier said than done, but don't skimp on people. Technology has its limitations. In the middle of a project, ask yourself whether current staffing levels will support their effective usage throughout the organization. If they won't, don't be afraid to suspend the project until business conditions improve.

M&A ACTIVITY

Business strategy types often don't like it when "operational" issues rear their ugly head into the mix. M&As are often supposed to close at the end of a quarter or year. Migrating data or integrating systems often stand in the way of these key dates and objectives. There's a tendency for some people to overlook data issues (or at least minimize them).

> Hiding known issues for fear of reprisals benefits no one in the long term.

Simon Says: How to Prevent Breaking Bad
Prioritize and be honest. Data quality might not be perfect post-merger, but get all the cards on the table. Hiding known issues for fear of reprisals benefits no one in the long term. Short-term pressures to close deals should not obviate the need for judicious reporting of data-oriented issues.

Idea 47: Creating Data Quality Reports That Matter
Dylan Jones

Endless profiling reports, column stats, and data quality metrics at an attribute, table, and system level ensue because generally, these are the easiest reports to create and appear to deliver excellent insight into the progress of the data quality project.

Although these reports do have value, the benefits are often

> To ensure that your team gets continued support and greater traction throughout the organization, you need to move beyond "canned" reports and deliver insight that means something to the wider business.

limited to the technical teams. To ensure that your team gets continued support and greater traction throughout the organization, you need to move beyond "canned" reports and deliver insight that means something to the wider business.

In short, you need to deliver reports that people in the business can really act on. To do this, you have no option but to model how the business fulfills services and products, integrate this with your data quality efforts, and create reports that link these worlds.

A personal example might help demonstrate this. I once met a progressive data quality team supporting a large telco in the UK. The members had identified a process failure in one of the fulfillment service areas where expensive equipment was not being returned to spares if a customer cancelled the order prior to contract sign-off. As a result, new equipment was provisioned, and the telco incurred considerable costs as a result.

If the data quality team had simply produced a series of canned data quality reports for each system that lay on the fulfillment information chain, the story would have been very dull indeed. As the data quality lead pointed out, profiling only told part of the story; it was the chain of events running through the many systems that resulted in the equipment becoming "stranded."

So, the first activity the team members did was to model the information chains and service chains through the various systems to combine data quality metrics with business metrics. They could now see how many orders were provisioned, which orders were at each phase, and which orders were coming back to spares. They could also report on defects along the information chain, down to the individual engineer or planner who had made the mistake.

A simple statistical process control (SPC) chart was created, and team members set to work on eliminating the root causes. From a business perspective, this was gold dust. Members could now take direct action to train planners and engineers, improve their business process, and create a more holistic improvement strategy.

Everything continued well, and the chart showed a steady drop in defects and a constant profit line, marrying equipment serviced to contracts signed off.

Then something interesting happened.

A developer in one of the systems that was used to fulfill the orders made a change that resulted in a data quality defect being introduced. Instantly, the team members witnessed a drop in signed-off revenue against equipment provisioned. They were able to instantly rectify the issue.

The key was marrying these two worlds, combining the business and data quality views. If you're just measuring data quality in isolation of how the business is performing, you run the risk of the following:

- Failing to demonstrate value of business change against data quality efforts
- Failing to trap errors that are not covered in your data quality rule set
- Failing to give the business and technical teams actionable insights

How are you reporting on data quality? Are you taking a big-picture view, or are you down in the trenches reporting on column stats and basic data quality metrics? What's working for you?

Part III: Data Governance

Relatively few organizations have reached a state of effective data governance—that is, they are concurrently and comfortably handling their management, data quality, and data stewardship. Although elusive, the benefits of effective data governance are hard to understate.

Many organizations mistakenly consider data governance to be a technical issue, best handled by IT departments. Yet, as the contributors show in this section, people issues actually drive a great deal of data governance. The contributors also dispel fallacies such as data governance being a discrete, one-time event or program. Rather, to truly effect meaningful change, data governance must be an ongoing process.

Idea 48: Step Away from the Data
Jill Dyché

Many organizations are launching data governance programs right now. It's actually pretty exciting to watch, particularly since no two data governance programs are exactly the same.

The crux of data governance is in policy-making for enterprise data. This means policies for supporting new regulatory and legislative mandates, policies for ensuring the data is correct, and policies for the way new business rules will be sanctioned cross-functionally. One policy that a lot of our clients is discussing is this: no one is allowed to touch the data.

> The real reason that so many companies have been tempted to have a "You touch it, you buy it" policy around their data is because they don't have the systems and processes in place to monitor what's being done to the data.

What? No one can touch data? Ever? I initially came to terms with this idea. Coming from a data warehousing background, I understood the attraction of housing cleansed data in a single, read-only repository for analytics.

But what happens when a customer calls the support center to update his address? Or when a manager in marketing wants to define new customer segments? Should the call center rep or segment manager make a notation and rely on someone from IT to do the dirty work? And what about issues like data correction, data latency, and metadata?

The real reason that so many companies have been tempted to have a "You touch it, you buy it" policy around their data is because they don't have the systems and processes in place to monitor what's being done to the data. If someone calls in to the call center to change his address and a third-party data provider subsequently modifies the new address back to the original one, no one may ever know. However, simple logging and version control capabilities could help a savvy data steward pinpoint the changes and correct the data if it goes bad. Data integration and data quality vendors are embracing new workflow tools for exactly this reason.

With the investments we're making in data governance—and that means investing the time to design it, launch it, and maintain it according to the company's practices and culture—we need to reconsider investing in enabling technologies to improve our data. At the end of the day, we shouldn't step away from the data. We should embrace it, kiss it on the cheek, and tell it that we love it.

Idea 49: Data, Data Quality, and Corporate Acquisitions
David Loshin

Typically when you use "data quality" and "corporate acquisitions" in the same sentence, you are referring to an operational aspect of data integration after the fact, such as merging multiple customer databases into a single customer data set. Alternatively, how can we look at data and data quality to help drive decisions about corporate acquisitions? I've been doing some thinking about this recently and thought I'd share some ideas.

First, what are the strategic objectives of a corporate (or product) acquisition? Drivers include these:

- Leveraging the acquired company's customer base for new customer acquisition
- Extension and growth of sales/volume to existing customers by extending the product line to include the acquired company's product and service lines
- Stabilization and strengthening of prices as a result of reducing competition within the same markets
- The ability to extend the company's brand across the products and services provided by the acquired company

From the information perspective relating to these drivers, determining whether it makes sense for company A to acquire company B depends on answering questions related to the drivers. As an example, when considering the aspect of revenue growth through new customer acquisition or same customer sales, here are some questions to ask:

- What is the size of our customer base? If company A anticipates growing the customer base, are there specific targets that are to be met, and will an acquisition help meet that goal the best way?

- What regions are served by our company, and what regions are served by our competitors? Is company A looking just to extend its geographic reach to places where it is currently not making a market, or does that company want to reduce competition and strengthen prices within highly competitive regions?

> In many cases, the challenge is to access information that is not available internally, or even more of a challenge, to extrapolate knowledge of what goes on outside the organization based on knowledge derived from within the organization.

- What is our market share, and what are our competitors' market shares? Does company A seek to grow its market share, and if so, which of the competitors is the best candidate?

- What percentage of our customers buys products from our competitors?

Of course, these and similar questions are answered using analyses performed using a combination of the company's internal data coupled with externally acquired data. This brings us to the two issues:

- Does the company have access to the right data to perform the analyses?

- Is the quality of the available data sufficient to lead to believable results?

Both of these questions lead to fundamental data quality directives associated with dimensions of data quality: availability, accuracy, timeliness, currency, and consistency. In many cases, the challenge is to access information that is not available internally, or even more of a challenge, to extrapolate knowledge of what goes on outside the organization based on knowledge derived from within the organization. For example, the company can attempt to calculate its market share based on the percentage of actual sales to sales situations; if the company did not make the sale, then someone else must have done so. If you know which competitor made the sale, you can add that specific sale to its market share.

Each case needs to be reviewed to determine where the data comes from and whether it meets the data quality objectives. In turn, this information can be used to answer the types of questions that would lead to a buy/no-buy decision.

Idea 50: Enterprise Ubuntu
Jim Harris

The strategic importance of collaboration is one of my favorite topics, but so much has been written about the need for it on enterprise initiatives such as data governance, MDM, and data quality that people are sick and tired of hearing about it. However, the key to success is the willingness of people to embrace collaboration. It's necessary for every organization to dissolve the political barriers that have historically separated their business units and people from each other.

Many people roll their eyes at me when I discuss collaboration. Some people, like Henry Oldcastle IV, even tell me to go sing "Kumbaya" someplace else because they have real work to do—their work, which is all that really matters to them.

In this Idea, I'm not singing "Kumbaya"; I'm discussing Ubuntu.

UBUNTU

Ubuntu is a word from the Bantu languages of southern Africa, which can be translated into English as "I am what I am because of who we all are."

> The key to success is the willingness of people to embrace collaboration.

"Ubuntu is the essence of being human," according to Desmond Tutu, who goes on to say:

Ubuntu speaks particularly about the fact that you can't exist as a human being in isolation. It speaks about our interconnectedness. We think of ourselves far too frequently as just individuals, separated from one another, whereas you are connected, and what you do affects the whole world. When you do well, it spreads out; it is for the whole of humanity.

Nelson Mandela has explained it this way:

Ubuntu does not mean that people should not enrich themselves. The question therefore is: Are you going to do so in order to enable the community around you to be able to improve?

ENTERPRISE UBUNTU

Many organizations view success as a zero-sum game. In other words, for one person or one business unit to succeed, someone else has to fail.

We think of ourselves far too frequently as just individuals, separated from one another; however, we are connected, and what we do affects the whole organization. This does not mean that we cannot have our personal agenda or prefer to act in the best interests of our business unit. The real question is this: are we going to do so to enable the entire interconnected enterprise around us to succeed?

Patrick Egan concluded his customer success story at the DataFlux IDEAS 2010 conference with the sage advice:

If you want to grow incrementally, then be competitive.

If you want to grow exponentially, then be collaborative.

Successful organizations view collaboration not only as a guiding principle, but as a call to action in their daily practices. Enterprise Ubuntu is an emphasis on the human side of business. Successful organizations have a united and shared purpose that is built upon open communication and enterprise-wide collaboration.

Successful organizations embrace and embody Enterprise Ubuntu.

Idea 51: Communications Gap? Or Is There a Gap Between Chasms?

David Loshin

Even when the IT folks are speaking the same language as their business partners, there seems to be a communications gap. And as I have seen recently with some of our clients, the gap is not always on the IT side. Although the SMEs on the business side are aware of the issues that directly affect their operational activities, they often are less aware of the more global issues that arise across the enterprise. In other words, the SMEs may be experts within their own business silo, but they're easily lost once they are asked to wander around the rest of the organization.

> Often the perspective is limited to the immediate impacts related to completing their own tasks, without considering if anyone downstream is also impacted.

This gap becomes apparent when soliciting opinions regarding organizational impacts associated with operational issues. Often the perspective is limited to the immediate impacts related to completing their own tasks, without considering if anyone downstream is also impacted. This is especially true in organizations with immature approaches to enterprise architecture. Because few individuals are tasked with the horizontal view, you rarely find someone who has one. Only when you wend your way up the food chain do you eventually find people with that strategic view. But at that level, it is likely that the individuals are far removed from the actual data.

Idea 52: Are You Really Ready for Data Governance?

Jill Dyche

Fall conference season has (mercifully) come to an end, and I can finally reflect on what I learned on my most recent tour of industry and vendor events.

(Editorial aside: I don't know about you, but I like Vegas, I love New Orleans, and if I ever see Orlando again, it'll be too soon. Note to conference organizers as you finalize your 2012 event planning: The Big Easy still needs our cash! Let's go back. The jambalaya's on me!)

Anyway, I've been speaking and writing a lot about data governance, and presentations at TDWI, SAS, Teradata, and various clients have placed me squarely in the crosshairs of people aiming for effective data governance programs. It's interesting to hear their

> Are you ready to get out of your comfort zone?

questions, particularly as they voice concerns about data governance adoption in their organizations. One question I get in almost every session is a variation of this one:

> *Alright Miss Fancy Pants, why is it that every time so-called experts talk about a major business initiative, they bring up change management? Why can't we just launch data governance without all the change management fanfare? Why can't we just 'get 'er done?'*

Answer: I don't know, why can't you? Or, more aptly, why haven't you? I'm not trying to be argumentative here, but

- My pants are just black wool crepe, trouser-cut, which I think is more understated than fancy.
- The most effective data governance programs are often also the most disruptive. And, simply put, disruption makes people nervous.

Professor Robert E. Quinn at the University of Michigan Ross School of Business writes about taking people out of their "normal states" (aka, their comfort zones) and painting a picture of what they need to do. In a seminal Harvard Business Review article in 2005 called "Moments of Greatness: Entering the Fundamental State of Leadership," Quinn described true leaders as ready to "venture beyond familiar territory to pursue ambitious new outcomes." If that's not data governance, I don't know what is.

After all, the "normal state" in most companies often means contradictory policies, multiple versions of the truth, absence of true data ownership, selective collaboration, and decision-making in a vacuum. Data governance is the opposite of all that.

"We couldn't afford to experiment with data governance," says Kevin Davis, director of research initiatives at a major southeast retailer. "We retained a consulting firm to teach us the foundational stuff, and we followed their advice. That included a lot of deliberate structure, education, evangelizing, and expectations management." Davis and his team faced the additional challenge of coupling their company's new data governance strategy with a major MDM technology acquisition. "We knew we only had one shot at getting it right," he says.

True, it's easier to avoid sticking your neck out. And in some cultures (particularly in high-tech companies), wholesale changes to policies and processes can actually begin from the bottom up. It's not only less disruptive, it demonstrates value to incent widespread adoption. Bottom-up data governance is a legitimate and proven approach. But at the end of the day, your strategy needs to include a plan to broaden governance beyond the initial domain. After all, if you're not sharing data across organizations and business processes, you don't need data governance.

According to Professor Quinn, change happens when someone is "jolted out of his comfort zone ... driven to clarify the result he wanted to create, to act courageously from his core values, to surrender his self-interest to the collective good, and to open himself up to learning in real-time."

Are you ready to get out of your comfort zone? Then maybe you are ready for data governance!

Idea 53: Data Quality Benchmarking
Dylan Jones

How do you know if your organization is maturing its data quality management principles in line with the wider industry?

One of our members posed a great question recently:

How do we know we're maturing in line with other companies when our progress feels glacial at times?

Benchmarking is never easy, particularly when the average company is blind to the need for data quality management.

One resource I recently used proved effective for helping a company benchmark its data quality maturity. It was the aptly titled the "Information Quality Management Capability Maturity Model"[iv] publication by Dr. Saša (Sasha) Baškarada. If you are responsible for data quality (and I'd add data governance and MDM into the mix), this book should be mandatory for your personal collection. It follows a "Chaotic—Reactive—Measuring— Managed—Optimizing" benchmarking process and provides some great insights into various quality frameworks and benchmarking principles.

I'm sure many practitioners will have their own views on what criteria should make up a benchmark, and you can debate endlessly about what should go into your own corporate benchmark—but from experience, Baškarada plugs a gap that many books I've read have missed.

> There's a whole rack of activities that lead to "quality data" that we typically already have the resources and wherewithal to tackle.

As a slight aside, one key point he addresses is that data quality management is built on a base of other techniques and disciplines we normally associate with broader data management and traditional IT processes. In other words, you can't lose sight of the "techie stuff" we often assume is taken care of.

What do I mean?

Well, in the early reactive phase, you might expect the focus to be on profiling, cleansing, and discovery, because this is an Information Quality benchmarking model after all. Instead, Baškarada focuses on benchmarks such as storage management, access control, security, and data modeling.

I like his approach for the simple reason that data quality management often begins with a deep dive into data, profiling, metrics, reporting, rule creation, monitoring, and cleansing. All the functions of classic data quality management often kick off first; as a result, many companies freeze until they have the capabilities in-house to perform the classic data quality activities.

However, as Baškarada rightly points out, there's a whole rack of activities that lead to "quality data" that we typically already have the resources and wherewithal to tackle. For example, there is a benchmark for "disaster management plans are in place for all storage facilities." This sounds like a typical IT function, but as data quality professionals, our role is to ensure the continuity of high-quality data. If that data disappears, never to return, surely we're missing a trick in not adding it to our benchmark of maturity?

I heard of one particular story in which a company had embarked on a data quality improvement strategy and an MDM initiative thrown in for luck. On the day after 9/11, the CEO demanded a full disaster recovery simulation as if one of its offices had been hit. It was discovered that the recovery tapes had not been sent via courier to the secure backup center. The loss of that much data would have been incalculable to the business, so the disaster brought home just how critical the "boring, IT-centric stuff" was to ongoing data quality.

If we, as data quality practitioners, are responsible for ensuring high-quality data and associated processes, we surely can't separate these functions out. It's all part of the same framework—or perhaps you have a different viewpoint?

Some might argue that the previous tale is classic IT territory—no need for data quality practitioners to play there. I'm not convinced. Sure, it's not our role to package up the tapes and ship them to the secure facility. But isn't it our role to ensure these processes exist, are well maintained, and routinely check out since the role of the data quality practitioner is to fundamentally protect the quality of any data assets that the organization depends on?

Perhaps the most interesting aspect of Baškarada's book for me was the many accounts from various employees in companies that provided benchmark data. It really makes you consider what people perceive as data quality and what we (in the data quality bubble) perceive to be our role.

Idea 54: Governance of "Unowned" Data
David Loshin

There are some deep issues associated with managing the quality of data sets with certain characteristics:

- The data originates from outside the organization's administrative domain.

- There is little influence over the processes in which the data sets are created.
- The data is generally available, but with no guarantees of usability.

As far as the organization is concerned, the data is basically "unowned"—there is no one within the organization with the authority over the data set. And that introduces an interesting challenge: how do you oversee the quality management when there is not assignation of authority? The answer lies in establishing governance policies related to authority and responsibility for this unowned data.

> At some point, someone must "officially" take responsibility for the data set.

The typical scenario for oversight is voluntary assignment—the person who first accessed the data set becomes the one who effectively owns it. Unfortunately, there are always going to be limits to what that individual can do, especially because other consumers within the organization reuse the data set. At some point, someone must "officially" take responsibility for the data set.

But even if data stewards are assigned to the data sets, there must be some directing authority who has the budget and resources allocated for addressing any existing data issues, soliciting additional data quality expectations and requirements, as well as addressing any issues that are uncovered as a result of use. This means that the data governance board must have a set of policies and procedures addressing the acquisition and management of unowned data to ensure it meets the quality needs of all internal data consumers.

Idea 55: It's Not About the Data, Stupid
Rich Murnane

I bet you'd never expect me to say, "It's not about the data." Being a data geek, I'm always talking about data, but there are times I have to realize why I spend most of my waking hours knee deep in all this data: to make the organizations I work for better at doing "business stuff": better at sales, marketing, human resources, financial management, risk management, travel management, whatever.

> Without firsthand experience seeing mature data management practices leading to better business stuff, organizations will continue to neglect their data.

Most organizations try to sell more widgets or do other business stuff, and data ends up being a pain in the neck for them. So why is data a pain in the neck? Organizations who find data painful do not manage their data in a mature fashion and have yet to "find religion." Why not? It's simple; they haven't yet seen the correlation between better data management and better business stuff. Without firsthand experience seeing mature data management practices leading to better business stuff, organizations will continue to neglect their data. The neglect will continue until bad stuff happens to their business stuff and the bad stuff is tied back to data. Once this happens, these folks start thinking about religion.

Becky Briggs of ARC was one of the presenters at a recent local DAMA chapter meeting. She took us through ARC's journey of "finding religion" by instituting data governance practices when standing up a new data warehouse and data aggregation business. Interestingly enough, it wasn't bad stuff that triggered the business's data management maturity; it was the recognition that if it didn't institute these practices at the start of this new venture, the venture wouldn't succeed. Briggs and the team at ARC have accomplished something few others I've spoken to have accomplished, and their story is quite impressive. If you have the chance to go to the Data Governance and Information Quality conference in San Diego at the end of June, you can sit in on Briggs's presentation and learn all about ARC's journey to better business stuff because of mature data management.

So, is it about the data? No. It's all about enabling your organization to do better "business stuff" through mature data management. With that said, maybe it is about the data after all...

Idea 56: Data-Driven Customer Churn

Dylan Jones

We recently moved, which resulted in various changes to contracts and services with utilities and telecom providers.

There have been three noticeable impacts arising from this seemingly straightforward activity:

- Serious data quality issues are common in the UK utility service providers I dealt with.
- These failures are directly hitting their bottom line.
- The providers don't want to know about the problems.

ONE HOME, MULTIPLE RECORDS

Having been involved with a number of data quality initiatives in several large UK utility organizations, I know that structurally they are typically constructed of multiple silos, often performing quite independent functions. Technology and business process design are intended to seamlessly link these disparate business units into one customer-facing organization.

My recent experience illustrates why we are still some way off from this scenario. I spent four weeks with one service provider trying to get two divisions of the same organization to talk to each other.

The result was complete stalemate. One division was adamant that our house would not be able to receive a new service because the information it had on the system indicated it was not feasible. The other division informed me that its information was more accurate than that of the other division but there was a fault on the line that meant it could not process the transfer order.

"Are you sure the information you have is correct?", I demanded, particularly because I was calling from the faulty line in question.

So each day for a month I'd call each business unit and try to get these folks to resolve their internal differences. I failed dismally until one day, miraculously, everything seemed to work, but I never found out which division actually resolved the issue.

However, I still received an automated phone call for several weeks (at 8 a.m.) from yet another department informing me that our fault was being worked on and a resolution was in the pipeline.

THE COMPLAINT PROCESS

This was not an isolated incident. I had issues with practically every supplier that needed to be updated about our move, and there were countless data quality issues. Names were spelled incorrectly, billing was incorrect, termination dates were wrong, terminations were unauthorized—the list goes on.

But the biggest problem I found was that actually providing feedback to these organizations could be extremely difficult. In one instance, I asked to speak to a more senior member of the organization so I could explain the problems I was having and why this would cause me to cease my service and become yet another customer churn statistic.

"No, it's not our policy to transfer you to more senior members of the support team"—hardly inspires you to fill out a complaints form, does it?

> The fact is that complaints are just a small sample of the total volume of issues that ultimately cause customer churn.

And that's if you can find a complaints form. Most of the websites I checked had no simple means of providing feedback so they could quickly learn from their mistakes and monitor the customer trends.

COMPLAINTS = CHURN = BOTTOM LINE = DATA QUALITY FOCUS

Finding data quality issues that have a demonstrable hit on the bottom line is not straightforward. Doing it well requires inside-out and outside-in consulting (that is, examining the data for obvious issues while running workshops and feedback sessions to figure out what is happening in the real world). In all the companies I have dealt with recently, mining the complaints data would be a perfect starting point for a data quality improvement initiative.

The fact is that complaints are just a small sample of the total volume of issues that ultimately cause customer churn. So you can bet whatever complaints you are receiving need to be scaled up to fully comprehend the "(frustrated) voice of the customer."

Where am I heading with all this?

Well, if I was tasked to improve data quality in one of these organizations, I'd start with what is causing my business to lose customers to competitors, because this is demonstrable and is clearly a strategic driver of any company.

It costs these organizations vast sums of marketing budgets to capture each new customer, and it no doubt costs a whole lot more to win back an ex-customer, so if you're trying to launch a data quality initiative, this surely has to be a great starting point.

IDEAS FOR DATA-DRIVEN UTILITY ORGANIZATIONS

Here are some obvious bullet-point actions for a UK telco or utility organization that is leaking customers right now:

- **Make it easier to provide feedback:** Create one simple URL (for example, *www.ourorg.com/feedback*) and promote this on your letterheads, your bills, your emails, your media ads, your call centers—everywhere you connect with consumers. Make the feedback form simple. If I'm a frustrated customer, don't make me fill out 15 fields; give me one box with an optional email or telephone for my contact details.
- **Mine the complaints system:** What are the trends? What causes the most frustration? Turn your data quality tools and profilers onto this gold mine of performance data. Get some actionable intelligence to help you focus your next steps.
- **Identify some quick wins:** What are the top issues that are causing customers to take their service and cash elsewhere? Speak to them, find out why, and truly understand the "voice of the customer."
- **Form a cross-organization working team:** This team should tackle the service, process, system, and data quality causes of the most serious issues hitting the bottom line.

You will notice that my last point does not focus solely on data quality improvement. That is because in most cases poor data quality is a symptom, not the cause.

Sure, three different departments having a different set of records for our account can be classified as a classic data quality issue, but what is the real cause of this? Poor data entry? Disparate applications that are not in-sync and in need of MDM? Lack of any sensible business process design? Inadequate staff training?

The cause of customer churn is rarely clear-cut, and I'm a firm believer that data quality teams should work in tandem with other service improvement teams to make holistic improvements that really stick.

Idea 57: "Chunks" of Data Governance

Joyce Norris-Montanari

What if I can't do the entire corporate data governance plan all at once? What happens then? What if I can only do data governance for one subject area or application at a time? For example, maybe our first implementation of data governance is only the customer subject area.

Obviously, we need a future vision as to what data governance should be at this organization. We also need to understand that the data governance plan can change as acquisitions are made and integration projects take root.

So, I am voting for "chunks" of data governance! Chunks could be by subject area (customer) or by application (ERP, customer management system, and so on). So, if I am doing chunks of data governance, would I still create all the goals, mission statements, value statements, and so on at a corporate level or just at a chunk level?

> We need a future vision as to what data governance should be at this organization.

Here are my thoughts:

- I'd create corporate business goals and detail the chunk I am currently implementing. The business goals could change over time, so make sure all the chunks equal the whole, and you can map each chunk back to the corporate business goals.
- I'd do the same for the value statement. Although the value may change with each chunk, everything should map back to the corporate value statement(s). I do hope you have more than one value statement for the data governance initiative.

- I don't think the mission statement for data governance would change if we chunk in the governance. However, it should be readdressed with each chunk implementation.

So, does this make data governance a program not a project?

Idea 58: The Data Quality Scorecard
David Loshin

Around our office, there has been a lively debate regarding the value of a visual scorecard for data quality. On the one hand, customers have gravitated toward the idea that you can provide direct feedback to data consumers regarding the measures of data quality. The idea resonates with the balance of our messaging that focuses on identifying and characterizing the impacts of poor data quality and how the criticality of certain types of underlying data issues can be communicated to business data consumers.

Certainly, the scorecard concept has been useful in a number of client engagements in a number of ways, with these specific examples:

- Socializing a value proposition for MDM policies.
- Defining acceptability thresholds for data set quality for data sets managed by stewards within a data governance program.
- Justifying the increased investment in data analysis tools, such as data profiling and other analytical tools.
- Identifying concrete steps for specific data improvement activities.

So from a strategic perspective, the use of a scorecard has yielded benefits in driving the data quality program forward. Although there is evidence of positive impacts of the use of a data quality scorecard, can we justify the scorecard as an end in itself, or is it just a means to jump-start the quality improvement program?

CONTRARIAN VIEW

Yes, there is some value in creating a data quality scorecard. Earlier, I hinted that there was some internal controversy within my company about the long-term value of a scorecard as a component of a data quality program. Here is the basic point: of what use is a scorecard? If it is used to measure known errors, it should motivate a specific action to eliminate the root cause of the introduction of each of the errors.

If you have not fixed the problem, your scorecard measures are probably not going to significantly change. If you have fixed the root cause, your expectation should be that the error won't show up anymore. In that case, your scorecard measure should also not change. The scorecard is useful only in triggering the remediation action, helping the data quality analyst figure out the source of the problem, and guiding the analyst in eliminating the root cause. In any other situation, you might think that the scorecard is not going to add a lot of value.

> What the analyst needs is not a scorecard per se but an interactive dynamic means for measuring compliance with defined business rules.

This is the contrarian argument: if scorecards are only useful in limited remediation scenarios, why allocate resources to build a scorecard? Allocate your staff time to fixing problems instead of measuring them.

TO SCORE OR NOT TO SCORE—THAT IS THE QUESTION

We might change our question from whether we should use a scorecard to, "What do you use a scorecard for?"

I implied that the data quality analyst can use the measurement and drill-down capability to do the root cause analysis—perhaps iteratively applying the measures to the data at various points along the information processing flow to determine the point at which the error occurred.

The drill-down can help to point out potential patterns of errors that are indicative of root causes. Providing an interactive capability would lend some degree of analytical agility.

What the analyst needs is not a scorecard per se but an interactive dynamic means for measuring compliance with defined business rules. And, of course, although this differs from a conceptual "visualization" approach from a scorecard, under the hood the rules engine and measurement methods are basically identical: define a rule, point the engine at some data, get a measure, display the results, allow for drilldown. This will satisfy the needs of the analyst for operational data quality investigations and for speeding the time for problems to be found and fixed.

There is only one problem remaining: in a lot of cases, the value of the scorecard was in communication of the value proposition to jump-start the data quality program. The use of the scorecard was for publicity—showing the existence and then the scale of the problems. Without the scorecard, some of the organizations would not have gotten buy-in for moving further. So it looks like we have a little bit of a conundrum.

EXPLOITING THE DATA QUALITY SCORECARD CONCEPT

Here's the problem: scorecards are good for initially communicating the value proposition to the right people in the organization—those who need to be shocked and awed by the existence, scope, and scale of the problem.

Those are the types of people who require "sight bites" (my own take-off on "sound bite") that allow them to rapidly review, internalize, and recognize the problem. They need the sizzle and are less interested in the steak.

The steak eaters are the operational data quality teams—the analysts and stewards who need to probe compliance with data expectations at various points along the way. That way they can find where the problem occurs and narrow down the place at which the errors are created.

Interestingly, to some people, there is effectively no difference between using the scorecard for reporting and using it for analysis. In fact, at a recent series of discussions, the data quality staff had effectively conflated the two concepts, using the term "scorecard" to mean both the high-level presentation and the analysis tool. Perhaps that is the best way to exploit the concept: transition a fancy method for visualization into the key component of an interactive data analysis process.

Idea 59: Finding the Common Thread
Joyce Norris-Montanari

I don't really sew, but I quilt periodically. Because I needed to do some mending, I got the machine out. It had been eight years since I had used this sewing machine, and some maintenance was required.

Much like a sewing machine, data needs servicing now and then. If you have a data governance initiative, ongoing auditing and maintenance should be part of that plan. Include things like these:

> Much like a sewing machine, data needs servicing now and then.

- Profile the data at specific intervals based on the business rules you have already gathered. This can be automatically set up, and the result can be fed to the data store for your data governance dashboard.
- Look for dollar amounts that are below or above a specific threshold.
- Recheck mailing address and email address for consistency and completeness.
- Run clustering algorithms to make sure all the Joyce records are the right Joyce.

If everything checks out, pat yourself on the back and don't forget to report the finding to management. Send out the report, and smile a lot at your dashboard. You may want to consider finding new ways to publish this data to the enterprise. There's nothing like reassuring the business partners on the accuracy of the corporate data!

If this doesn't work, I am taking it to a professional (the machine, that is).

Idea 60: Data Governance and the Occasional Vow of Celibacy
Jill Dyché

Recently the chair of a data governance council at a bank asked for my thoughts on how to handle dormant data. The data—some cryptic financial rollup tables that hadn't been accessed in a few months—was taking up space on the data warehouse. More importantly, it would soon be subject to a major financial metadata effort. My client didn't want his staff spending time defining data that no one was using.

When the topic of decommissioning data comes up, I think about Information Lifecycle Management (ILM). This is the management and storage of data as it changes over time, from its initial creation through its eventual use and disposition. We've talked quite a bit with clients about data being dynamic and having a life cycle. We call this life cycle the data supply chain.

I asked my client a series of questions about the data. Why was it loaded onto the data warehouse in the first place? Did it map to critical business requirements? Who'd requested it?

> Sometimes you've got to take something away to recognize its real value.

What business processes did it support? How latent was it? Ultimately, after some discussion, I recommended that my client pull the data from the data warehouse and archive it. Then we'd sit back and await the backlash.

A risky move? You bet. I compare this strategy to the one used in the Aristophanes play *Lysistrata*. As you'll remember from high school English, in *Lysistrata*, the women of Greece decide en masse to withhold sex from their husbands until there was an end to the Peloponnesian War. It was the ultimate power play and gave the term "cease fire" a whole new meaning.

A week later my client received an email from a data analyst in the finance department inquiring about the missing data. It seemed as if this analyst used the data to create quarterly top-line measure reports for the CFO. She'd just returned from a three-month sabbatical and wondered what had happened to her tables.

This conversation resulted in the addition of two new guiding principles for the data governance council:

- Usage of the data on the warehouse would be regularly monitored.
- Data unused for a period of four months or longer would be archived unless the data steward requested an exception.

These new guiding principles invited a new level of—dare I say—intimacy with less visible data by data stewards who had until then been focused on high-profile or heavily queried tables. But just because the data wasn't widely used didn't mean it wasn't beholden to the standard policy-making and oversight processes established by the data governance council.

The lesson? Sometimes you've got to take something away to recognize its real value. Just ask those randy Greeks.

Idea 61: The Long Road to Becoming "Data Aware"
Rich Murnane

Intelligent data management is predicated on people. And intelligent people understand there is more to data than just building an application that stores data in a database. There are those who realize there is more to data than just managing database backups generating a few reports for a manager. Granted, this target audience is currently much smaller than that of the army of operational database administrators and developers you'll find at most IT shops. What I continue to see (and what happened to me) is that, sooner or later, these operational IT folks become data aware and cognizant that there is more to this data thing than what meets the eye.

So, what exactly is "data aware?" It's the realization that now your organization's data is in fact an asset of your organization, just like the products and services you supply and the people who make your organization different from competitors. Like other assets of an organization, data assets need attention—far beyond that which can be given from operational staff that build and support applications because those folks are busy focusing on just that.

> Intelligent data management is predicated on people.

My road to becoming data aware could be best described as fumbling my way through various IT roles that focused on data. Over the years, I've worked as a data analyst, database developer, database administrator, data "this," and data "that." About five years ago or so, I was presented the opportunity to be one of the primary designers and developers of a cool new application. The project started off like most others; it was a good idea, we built a proof of concept, and we had some smart people who wanted to make a difference by making one particular business process much quicker (primary objective).

At some point, the folks on the team realized the power behind this new tool that had data quality processes built in from day one. Once deployed, the tool allowed our sales teams to respond to client requests significantly faster (listed in the requirements documents), with better and more consistent results (not listed in the requirements documents). The centralized database made it easy to build operational reports to see what was going on with each business unit as well as build high-level reports on what was going on throughout the organization as a whole. It didn't take long, but I went from being an operational IT staff member to data aware in a matter of a few months—and since arriving I've decided to never go back.

Regardless of the role you play in an organization, if you're reading this Idea, you've either arrived or started your journey to become data aware. It's likely that you recognize data has become significantly important to your organization and to the world around you. Keep in mind, however, statistically speaking, chances are most of the other people on your staff are not yet data aware. Few organizations have recognized the value of being data aware, and if you're in a shop that isn't data aware, it's going to be your job to help people understand its benefits.

I still have a ton to learn on my journey, but I've picked up a thing or two over the years that I'm eager to share. I'm excited to be part of the community, and I'm going to do my best to contribute to you and your organization's journey to becoming data aware.

Idea 62: Formal Versus Informal Data Governance
Phil Simon

For a long time now, I've wanted to write about data governance. I've become increasingly intrigued with the term over the past two years. In particular, one question has baffled me:

Why has it taken me so long to hear about it?

As much as I live in a vacuum, as a formal term, "data governance" has only entered the zeitgeist recently. But what about solid data management practices? Organizations cared about data quality, management, and policies before people started the term, right? In other words, what about informal data governance?

It turns out that I'm not the only one asking this question. In a short post on her blog,ᵛ my friend Jill Wanless asks this:

> Can data governance be informal? Is there such a thing? Doesn't formalization make up a key (and critical) component of governance?
>
> Isn't informal data governance not data governance at all, but a hugely expensive and time-consuming (and mind-numbing) approach to getting people to buy in? [Text slightly modified from original post.]

Let's look at the viability of formal and informal data governance.

I have two opinions about informal data governance: one optimistic and one not so much. Let's be nice first. Yes, informal data governance exists. Employees and other agents of an organization need not have everything codified. They can recognize practices not aligned with the organization's best interests; they simply don't need formal data governance to make recommendations and changes to redress data-oriented issues. Employees will go above and beyond the norm, proactively taking steps to ensure that their organization—and folks at all levels—have accurate information on which to make important business decisions. Although not everyone has the same skills and mentality, at least no one is actively taking steps to undermine the organization's data governance efforts.

> I know of some companies that would struggle for many reasons, even with formal data governance mechanisms.

Now, it's time for the pessimist in me. Informal data governance will never fly because people only do what they're explicitly told to do—and sometimes, they don't even do that. (This I know from years of experience with difficult end users in organizations rife with internal battles.) Although no one is intentionally sabotaging systems, applications, and data, people will only follow strict policies and procedures. They will not look beyond their immediate lines of sight; they are only concerned with covering their areas, pleasing their bosses, and addressing their issues. Needless to say, there isn't a great deal of cooperation in organizations like these. Can someone say "dysfunctional culture"?

SIMON SAYS

I have intentionally used two extreme scenarios here. I sincerely doubt that many organizations out there fall squarely into either camp. To be sure, people in different departments, divisions, and areas adhere to informal data governance practices better than others.

I know of no guarantees here. I just can't imagine certain organizations getting away with informal data governance. Conversely, I know of some companies that would struggle for many reasons, even with formal data governance mechanisms. I just don't see a silver bullet here. C-level executives can insist upon whatever they want, but it's the people at the lower rungs of the organization who will effect these visions.

Idea 63: Retrograde Organizational Motion
Jim Harris

Enterprise initiatives such as data governance, MDM, and data quality all face a common challenge: they require your organization to take on a significant and sustained change management effort. Despite being the most common phenomenon in the universe, change is almost universally resisted, making most of us act as if change is anything but common. We get complacent with the way things are, and it's always easier to stay the current course than it is to start moving in a new direction.

In my experience, the change management aspects of enterprise initiatives are either overlooked or trivialized. The usual result is that after the organization expends a significant amount of time, effort, and money, the deliverables of the new enterprise initiative are not widely adopted.

I have witnessed enterprise data warehouses fail to replace spreadmarts, MDM central repositories fail

> To overcome this inertial resistance to change, you must intentionally create a slippery slope at the beginning of the initiative.

to replace data silos, and data governance policies fail to be implemented and enforced. Although it's common for technology to be blamed for these failures, more often than not a fundamental flaw in enterprise initiatives is poor change management.

Retrograde motion is movement in the direction opposite to the movement of something else. Retrograde organizational motion is movement in the direction opposite to the movement of the organization's status quo. Change management is about adjusting the corporate culture to first accept the merits of retrograde organizational motion—and then start moving in that new direction.

Isaac Newton's First Law of Motion states this: "An object in motion tends to stay in motion. An object at rest tends to stay at rest." Newton defined inertia as the corresponding resistance that an object has against any attempted change in its motion.

To overcome this inertial resistance to change, you must intentionally create a slippery slope at the beginning of the initiative. If it is too difficult to get started, organizational inertia (aka the status quo) will win. Change management efforts are about building and sustaining the change momentum until organizational inertia works with you instead of against you, so that once the necessary changes are in motion, they stay in motion.

Are you ignoring the physics of retrograde organizational motion in your enterprise initiatives?

Idea 64: The Case For and Against "Studs and Duds"
Phil Simon

With football season starting tonight, I thought that I'd tie together two ostensibly disparate topics: data management and fantasy football. I'll be the first to admit that I have not assembled the most balanced roster in the history of the "sport." Loading up on elite players and filling out the rest of the cast with primarily $1 and $2 players is a strategy often referred to as "studs and duds."

Although I could write for hours about the ins and outs of fantasy football, I'd like to switch gears and ask one simple question: does a studs and duds strategy make sense for internal data management? In other words, can you spend most of your organization's internal budget on a few superstars and staff other positions with average folks?

Note that I am intentionally neglecting the elephant in the room: data management, governance, and quality should not be confined to an individual department. Everyone needs to understand the importance of these concepts—and the downstream impacts of ignoring them.

THE CASE FOR

Studs can identify and fix data-related problems with speed, precision, and tremendous skill. They can easily pinpoint the people, processes, interfaces, and applications causing issues. Rather than being merely reactive, however, they proactively forecast potential issues. They ask logical questions before, not after.

For all these reasons, studs are worth their weight in gold. While the unemployment rate in many countries is quite high, true rock stars are always in great demand. As such, paying them above-market wages is not only required, it makes good business sense. A few studs can obviate the need for expensive external consultants and give senior management greater confidence in the data on which it makes key business decisions.

The essence of this strategy can be stated as follows: people always make mistakes, and having a bunch of "average" folks is probably not going to manifest a "sleeper" who can minimize damage to a project.

THE CASE AGAINST

Studs can only do so much. By staffing key positions with employees paid at or below average wages, the organization runs the risk of employee indifference and a resultant decline in data quality and integrity. What's more, average pay may result in increased attrition which, in turn, also causes more data-oriented issues.

> Pay people a solid wage, but let unaffordable folks walk.

New employees invariably have learning curves, even on widely used systems. Can someone say "vicious cycle"?

Under the "anti-stud" philosophy, money spent on studs is simply better utilized when dispersed across the entire organization. More money is available for training, bonuses, and other carrots designed to promote a loyal, long-term workforce. Fewer issues should result because, quite frankly, people know what they're doing.

SIMON SAYS

There's no one right view on studs and duds. A third strategy (in management, fantasy football, and life) is to embrace moderation. This means staffing your organization with a solid group of folks capable of doing their jobs. Pay people a solid wage, but let unaffordable folks walk. The whole is greater than the sum of its parts.

Moreover, remember that people are only part of the data management world. Organizations with superior processes and technology may be able to get by without studs. However, there's a flip side to that coin. If a process or technology breaks, will the duds have the skills to identify the problem and affected records? Will they be able to implement the fix in a timely fashion?

Part IV: Master Data Management

Sadly, many organizations do not maintain master records on employees, customers, vendors, and products. Perhaps this would not cause major problems if most organizations managed their data well. Part I showed that this is rarely the case.

As a consequence of not maintaining master records, organizations often have to spend far too much time and money answering fundamental questions such as these:

- How many employees work here?
- Which invoices were paid, sent, and cashed?
- What do we sell?
- To whom do we sell it?

This section explores issues related to the relatively recent field of MDM. The contributors weigh in on MDM best practices and offer essential advice for organizations struggling to find the Golden Record.

Idea 65: On Screwdrivers and Product Data

David Loshin

Ever walked around the screw department at your local hardware super mega-store? Isn't it incredible how many types of metal fasteners there are? Wood screws, sheet metal screws, machine screws. Lag bolts, eye bolts, elevator bolts. Interestingly, there are lots of different names for the same things:

- Hex bolts are also known as hex cap screws.
- Socket screws are also referred to as Allen head screws.
- Shoulder bolts are also called stripper bolts.

Here is a small list of different types of head styles:

- Phillips pan head
- Slotted pan head
- Square drive pan head
- Phillips flat head
- Slotted flat head
- Square drive flat head
- Phillips oval head
- Slotted oval head
- Phillips truss head
- Phillips pan head self-drilling
- Phillips flat head self-drilling
- Hex washer head
- Hex washer head self-drilling

By the way, the screws come in a variety of materials—zinc-plated steel, stainless steel, bronze. The steel comes in different grades, according to different diameters. The diameters could be measured in inches or using metric length measures.

I hope you get the point. For what we believe to be a relatively straightforward concept ("screw"), there are many different descriptions, characteristics, and attributes that must be used to differentiate one type from another.

Now here is the question: how many different ways are there to represent a screw? And how can you even tell if a product "description" is actually a screw? Here are some examples:

- 5/16–24 1/2 × 3/16 hex jam nut
- 3/8–16 11/16 × 15/64 hex-heavy
- RD HD steel machine screw
- 6–32 × 1 3/4" steel slotted
- 10–32 × 1 1/8" steel slotted
- RD HD steel pre-assem. screw
- Allen socket HD cap screw
- 5/16–18 × 1 5/8 hex head
- 5/16–18 × 7/8 hex head steel
- 5/16–18 × 3/4 hexagonal

Each of these examples describes some kind of fastener product, but even within the same data set, there are going to be a number of ways that each one maps to some standard set of characteristics that identify the represented object. In other words, the name of the object is not only its name. It represents so much more. For instance, it also carries embedded and potentially encoded identifying information. Idea 67, "Product Data Is Different," continues this discussion.

Idea 66: Facebook and Common Sense
Joyce Norris-Montanari

My niece just became a fan of "The problem with common sense … is that it's not that common." When I saw this message show up on her Facebook Wall, I started thinking about how I assume that everyone must know how vital data integration and MDM are to an organization. I mean, isn't it common sense?

Wouldn't it even be better if the MDM software, data quality software, and data profiling software were on the same platform? They could share a repository (truly integrated), with one software installation (one engine with

> Some vendors put lipstick on a pig: they buy software, each with its own repository, and then cover up their lack of integration by putting an interface over the top of all three products.

multiple options), and one user interface. Wouldn't that be great for our data management initiative?

With all the acquisitions going on right now, true integration with the MDM software, ETL tool, and data quality/profiling tool may be an impossible task. Some vendors put lipstick on a pig: they buy software, each with its own repository, and then cover up their lack of integration by putting an interface over the top of all three products. It's not the best thing to do in the long run, but it does sell those products together.

I think my common sense would tell me to ask the following questions:

- Does each software type (MDM, data quality, ETL, and data profiling) require different user ID/password combinations? If so, the integration may not be where you want it to be.
- How does the MDM software use the data quality metadata? Do I have to run a routine to share?
- How do I report, manage, and audit the platform?

I guess I will go see what my niece is a fan of today!

Idea 67: Product Data Is Different
David Loshin

In Idea 65, we started to examine some characteristics of product data by looking at both the name data and the characteristics of types of items and their integration as part of the name.

By looking at the example of the variety of metal screws and other fastener-related objects, we started to see how variation in the name could lead to confusion:

- **RD HD steel machine screw:** I suspect that RD HD means "round head," and it is a machine screw, but there are not associated measurements or other attributes.
- **6–32 × 1 3/4″ steel slotted:** This is a screw that has a slotted drive style, a 6/32 size, and a length of 1 ¾ inches. I'm not sure about any of the other attributes, although a Google search pointed me to Amazon, where I found a machine screw described with these characteristics.

In any event, product data is different from part data. Names are descriptive; their parts reflect common (yet unstandardized) abbreviations and acronyms, there is some order and structure associated with the name components, and different representations are likely to exist depending on the originating source.

> Whether the company sells consumer products, is a manufacturer, or even is within an organization's own procurement processes, there is a need to create, manage, and store product data.

On the other hand, a large percentage of businesses somehow deal with products. Whether the company sells consumer products, is a manufacturer, or even is within an organization's own procurement processes, there is a need to create, manage, and store product data. Wouldn't it be nice if we could manage that information in a single place?

Idea 68: Learning from the Change Agents: Change Management for MDM

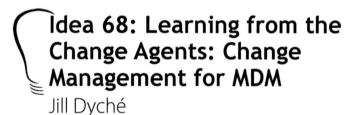

Jill Dyché

In our recent crop of MDM and customer data integration (CDI) projects, we've seen firsthand how company cultures support change—or how they don't. Institutionalizing MDM means introducing new processes, new policies, and new technology solutions. It mandates business involvement. It changes people's paradigms and maybe their jobs. Heck, most times an organization's vocabulary has to change.

Even for a relatively inarguable proposition like formally managing a company's master data, defining that data around common definitions and policies, integrating it from across siloed organizations and systems, and propagating it to the systems and users who need it, a certain degree of change readiness is required. For changes in the way a company manages its information assets, transformational leadership might even be in order.

For those of us "on the ground" who don't have time to take a human factors class or submit ourselves to protracted surveys about our own motivations—a hearty shout-out to all my fellow INTJs[4] and you Arrangers out there, you know who you are!—here are a few qualities we've seen in companies that reflect solid leadership capabilities and help propel the socialization of MDM to a cross-functional audience of business and IT constituents:

> Even for a relatively inarguable proposition like formally managing a company's master data, defining that data around common definitions and policies, integrating it from across siloed organizations and systems, and propagating it to the systems and users who need it, a certain degree of change readiness is required.

- **Define the boundaries of MDM:** We have a couple clients who suffer from what we call "Bright, Shiny Object Syndrome." This means they rally around new terms and are the first to jump on any bandwagon, even if it threatens to run them over. Defining what MDM is—and what it isn't—can sober up the most eager group of fad-happy trend chasers.
- **Expect fear:** Introducing CDI and personal information management (PIM) can threaten those in charge of incumbent technologies. There are always potential stakeholders who, getting a whiff of the MDM smoke on the horizon, circle the wagons and refuse to share information or requirements. And I've written before about the change-agent executives willing to take them on.
- **Use success stories:** People fundamentally resist change because they can't imagine its corollaries. By painting a picture of what MDM success looks like at companies that have delivered

---

4. Introverted iNtuitive Thinking Judging, or INTJs, are perfectionists with a seemingly endless capacity for improving upon anything that takes their interest. What prevents them from becoming chronically bogged down in this pursuit of perfection is the pragmatism so characteristic of the type: INTJs apply (often ruthlessly) the criterion "Does it work?" to everything from their own research efforts to the prevailing social norms. This in turn produces an unusual independence of mind, freeing the INTJ from the constraints of authority, convention, or sentiment for its own sake. See *http://typelogic.com/intj.html*.

it—Intuit, Sun Microsystems, Amgen, Bell Canada, and ING Insurance Americas are all great examples—you can do a lot to put people's natural change resistance to rest.

Ultimately, whether we're talking about MDM or the evolving role of IT in business, we need to start addressing people's personal stake in the proposed change. It might only be a matter of a couple well-placed case studies and an "aha" moment.

Idea 69: The Future of MDM: Create an Architecture That Is Enterprise-Centric

Joyce Norris-Montanari

I was visiting with a company the other day about a consulting position, and lo and behold, the MDM initiative was brought up. It's not that I'm knocking MDM, but the business intelligence assessment suggested that this company start with a small (but foundation ready) data warehouse, with data marts, and analytics on the financial subject area. The problems with the data increased as the project began requirements and design.

> If we create master data for only one purpose—the data warehouse—we have done the enterprise an injustice.

This is a siloed environment, as many are, and the data was not assessed in the beginning.

Anyway, long story short, the vendor suggested MDM as the answer. I agree that a store of customer/product data is required. However, if we create master data, shouldn't we use it as an enterprise asset and not just for the data warehouse?

If we create master data for only one purpose—the data warehouse—we have done the enterprise an injustice. Here are some of the issues I see:

- The source systems may have incomplete customer/product data that does not match the MDM store.
- If the source systems are not changed to incorporate the master data, things could get out of sync. This requires data governance and some good MDM practices.

- If the enterprise does not accept the master data as the "truth" (and the answer to redundant/incomplete data), the data warehouse may not match the source system data.

The future of MDM should be directed by the enterprise, using the best MDM methodologies, data governance practices, and tools!

Take a deep breath when embarking on an MDM initiative, and make the right choice for the enterprise, not just the data warehouse.

Idea 70: The Semantic Future of MDM
Jim Harris

In *Master Data Management*, David Loshin writes:

Master data objects are those core business objects used in the different applications across the organization, along with their associated metadata, attributes, definitions, roles, connections, and taxonomies.

Common examples of master data include customers, employees, vendors, suppliers, parts, products, locations, contact mechanisms, profiles, accounting items, contracts, and policies.

Master Data Management (MDM) incorporates business applications, information management methods, and data management tools to implement the policies, procedures, and infrastructures that support the capture, integration, and subsequent shared use of accurate, timely, consistent, and complete master data.

This book remains my favorite resource for understanding MDM as we know it today.

SIMPLIFYING THINGS FOR THE PURPOSES OF DISCUSSION

First, let's simplify the definitions so we can differentiate master and transaction data:

- Master data is an abstract description of real-world entities.
- Transaction data is an abstract description of real-world interactions involving two or more of these entities.

Now let's use a simple (and fictional) example of MDM as we know it today:

> *Michelle Davis purchases a life insurance policy from Vitality Insurance.*

In this example, Michelle Davis (customer), the life insurance policy (product), and Vitality Insurance (vendor) are all master data objects, and the premium payments that Michelle Davis sends to Vitality Insurance exemplify the transaction data involved. Currently, both master and transaction data management is focused entirely on the perspective of Vitality Insurance, which, for the most part, does make sense.

Both the vendor and product master data objects used in this example are owned by Vitality Insurance because it is the vendor and it makes the product being sold. Vitality Insurance also owns the transaction data because that is how the company makes money—especially if Michelle Davis lives a relatively long life. However, Vitality Insurance doesn't own the other master data object in this example—namely, its customer Michelle Davis.

But Vitality Insurance would claim (no pun intended) to own the master data that describes Michelle Davis. It is this particular aspect that I will focus on in this discussion about the future of MDM. This aspect is not only the most significant challenge facing MDM today, but also the fundamental flaw that the future of MDM must resolve.

COPIES OF YOUR CUSTOMERS

It can be easily argued that achieving a single view of your customers is one of the fundamental goals of an MDM implementation. A single customer view allows your organization to understand how many customers you actually have and what the most "accurate, timely, consistent, and complete" data you actually have available to describe those customers.

However, attempting to achieve that goal is fraught with complexities. The larger your organization and the longer it has been in business, the greater the likelihood you have many disparate systems for storing and managing master data. That's why your organization probably suffers from inconsistent (or a total lack of) standards and ownership for all your master data objects, not just the customer object.

So many (and potentially conflicting) customer definitions and so many (and potentially redundant) copies of customer master data exist throughout the enterprise that MDM has become a daunting challenge.

Achieving a single customer view is the holy grail of today's MDM and is often referred to as creating the "golden copy" of each unique customer.

EVEN THE "GOLDEN COPY" IS STILL JUST A COPY

All data (master and transaction) is an abstraction. Creating golden copies is an attempt to perfect the abstraction, which remains disconnected from reality.

Even the best maintained golden copies still suffer from the digital distance that exists between these internal abstract descriptions and the external real-world entities that they are attempting to describe.

Nothing can change the fact that the text string "Michelle Davis" is only an abstract description of the human being whose name is currently Michelle Davis. Even if near real-time updates modify the text string as "Michelle Davis-Donovan" after Michelle Davis marries Michael Donovan in a beautiful seaside wedding, the same digital distance remains as a fundamental flaw in our current MDM world view. The inconvenient truth is that this real-world event was not simply a partial concatenation of two text strings swimming in a beautifully maintained digital sea of information within the world-class MDM system of Vitality Insurance.

ATTACK OF THE (DIGITAL) CLONES

Let's switch the perspective of this discussion to your perspective. No, I don't mean *your perspective* either as someone working on an MDM solution for your organization or as someone working for a vendor selling MDM solutions. I mean your individual and personal perspective.

How many companies currently view you as a customer? How many companies have previously viewed you as a customer at one or more times in the past? How many copies of your personal information (your master data) do you think exist within the databases and file systems of all the companies that you have ever done business with in your entire life? Don't forget to count all the companies that obtained your personal information indirectly from the companies that you directly provided your personal information to. (In our example, imagine all the third-party companies to which Vitality Insurance sends Michelle Davis's personal information to assess her insurance risk.) I refer to all these copies of your master data as your digital clones.

Now imagine how many of your digital clones still look like you. In other words, how many have your current postal addresses? Email addresses? Telephone numbers? How many of your digital clones have all your relevant personal information? How many of them don't know how old you are? How many of them don't know how many times you have been married or how many children you currently have? Would you even recognize all your digital clones if you saw them today?

Now imagine you are a customer of Vitality Insurance. It has implemented a world-class MDM system. Therefore, it is maintaining an accurate, timely, consistent, and complete golden copy of your customer master data. But what about all the other companies you do business with? That is the fundamental flaw of MDM today—the current focus is entirely on companies (Vitality Insurance) and not on individuals (Michelle Davis).

Why is your personal information being managed by anyone other than who owns it?

THE PERSONAL DATA LOCKER

In his excellent book *Pull: The Power of the Semantic Web to Transform Your Business*, David Siegel discusses the concept of the personal data locker, which will be your secure online account that stores all your personal information, where it will be managed by who truly owns it—you.

You will grant permission to access the relevant aspects of your personal information to the vendors and other service providers with which you conduct business. In most cases, the only personal information released will be your unique identifier (your OpenID or i-name). Please note: these are only examples. You will view all the transaction data connected to your master data—or requesting your verification to connect. For those familiar with online banking, imagine something similar to (but more advanced than) the way e-bills work in online bill pay. You will run your own personal MDM system. You will maintain the accurate,

> The most important aspect of the future of MDM is transitioning the management of master data to the real-world entities that actually own the data, thereby virtually eliminating both the abstraction and the digital distance undermining MDM today.

timely, consistent, and complete single view of your master data. There will be no copies (golden or otherwise) of your personal information. All your digital clones will be deleted.

THE SEMANTIC FUTURE OF MDM

The semantic web is a disruptive paradigm shift that will impact more than just the future of MDM. However, the semantic web is still in its nascent phase. Although it is rapidly evolving, it will take more time not only before everything necessary is in place, but for the defenders of the status quo to stop trying to fight the future. The semantic web is also about much more than just simply cloud computing and software as a service (SaaS), both of which generate a lot of industry buzz today.

There are even some vendors already beginning to offer new MDM "solutions" where master data moves into the cloud. However, these apparent early adopters are still missing the fundamental flaw underlying MDM today:

It is not simply that master data needs to move into the cloud.

The most important aspect of the future of MDM is transitioning the management of master data to the real-world entities that actually own the data, thereby virtually eliminating both the abstraction and the digital distance undermining MDM today. When this transition finally happens, organizations will be able to focus on managing the data they truly own—transaction data and only the master data that describes the organization and the core business objects it actually owns (its products). In the semantic future of MDM, organizations will stop wasting time and money attempting to manage data they do not own.

Idea 71: The Future of MDM: Master Policy Management?
David Loshin

Although the desire for a unified view is a strong one, there may be situations that prevent the physical consolidation yet can still benefit from layered master data services. For example, there may be legal or logistic restrictions from copying data from one location to another (such as due to jurisdictional regulation of data privacy, or perhaps the volumes are too great to stream across lower-bandwidth networks in a timely fashion). In these cases, it appears that the traditional "single source of truth" style of MDM is basically out of the question.

However, as the thought processes for establishing a business case for MDM mature, we are starting to see where the desire for the unified view is not completely dependent on an instantiation of a single consolidated repository. Instead, in these situations the business needs are supported by the availability of master data services implementing consistent information policies across an extended enterprise.

> We are starting to see where the desire for the unified view is not completely dependent on an instantiation of a single consolidated repository.

For example, individual personal records not being copied across jurisdictional boundaries does not preclude the communication of aggregated information. Furthermore, the rolled-up data from the various regions is valid, *as long as the methods for aggregation are consistent across all those regions.*

As another example, if you need to determine if a customer record already exists, you can package and broadcast the identifying information to each data environment, which you can then poll for a search and match. You can share all intermediate results with the requestor, and if an existing record is found at any of the locations, you can notify the initiating process that a potential match does exist, even if you can't provide the actual record. That process can then determine whether it's appropriate to ask the customer if he already has established a relationship.

In other words, certain aspects of the business needs are met through the consistent application of master information policies. These are dependent on some of the same basic features of any MDM implementation: common master data models, well-defined standards for reference data, and common master services. However, the consistent application of policies can be done both in the presence of a unified repository or as a federated collection of common repositories.

Idea 72: The Future of MDM: Enterprise Waste Removal

Dylan Jones

I seem to spend a lot of my time lately talking about the need for companies to understand the information chains that meander through their organization.

The information chain is still a poorly understood entity. It's responsible for delivering practically all the services of the modern organization yet is rarely managed and governed correctly in most organizations I visit.

Part of the reason for this is education, governance, resources—the usual culprits. But perhaps the biggest issue is the sheer complexity of even modest information chains.

I recently delivered a workshop to help a fairly small business team document the information chains that flowed into and out of their department. Three days of white board brainstorming demonstrated to the team members uncovered just how little they knew about the information under their control. The resulting information chains demonstrated just how far and wide their data traveled and what impact their defects could cause.

> MDM creates lean information chains, which is a good thing for internal and external customers.

One of the most useful (and simple) tools for the data quality professional is the time value map. This tool complements the information chain by identifying the wasteful processes that span the chain. It also benchmarks the chains across the organization, enabling you to target areas of the business that will directly lead to greater customer satisfaction, cost reduction, and many other strategic drivers that will keep data quality budgets intact.

So what does all this have to do with MDM, you may ask? MDM is set to change the future of many organizations by significantly reducing the complexity and length of information chains. In short, MDM creates lean information chains, which is a good thing for internal and external customers.

By centralizing information using typical MDM strategies, an organization reduces the distance data has to travel and the defects collected along the way. It can reduce time traps such as batch processing, and there is far less wasteful processing across the enterprise. This, of course, requires more than just technology. None of the gains can be made if the organization fails to re-engineer its information chains, and this requires a change in working habits and service design. I know of several large corporations that still cling onto their disparate legacy systems instead of switching to the new MDM architecture. Fear and politics ensure that highly complex, wasteful information chains persist.

However, based on the installations of MDM that I've witnessed, the performance gains far outweigh trepidations of moving forward into the unknown.

Idea 73: PMP and the MDM Project
Joyce Norris-Montanari

I'm studying to take my project management professional (PMP) certification exam. I've decided that because I've done project management for business intelligence and data integration projects for the past 20 years, I should have the certification to go with the experience. Now, you would think that with all this experience, this exam would be easy, but it won't be.

Because I'm studying so hard, I thought it would be a great idea to compare what I've learned to what I do in an MDM project.

Project management is composed of five processes:

- **Initiating:** Start
- **Planning:** Plan
- **Executing:** Do
- **Monitoring and controlling:** Check and act
- **Closing:** End

Based on the project manage processes, our MDM project would include the following:

- **Gathering requirements:** Initiating
- **Creating a feasibility study based on the requirements:** Initiating

- **Developing a project charter and scope:** Initiating
- **Planning risk and mitigation:** Planning
- **Planning architecture and design:** Planning
- **Planning implementation (resources, hardware, software):** Planning
- **Integration design:** Executing
- **Data modeling:** Executing
- **Metadata creation:** Executing
- **Integrating data:** Executing
- **Planning ongoing maintenance and enhancements:** Planning, monitoring, and controlling
- **Close and create new phase:** Closing

The way the Project Management Institute (PMI) thinks you should manage a project and the way we would handle our MDM project are similar. In fact, PMI includes every task we would perform in some part of the project management framework. Because MDM is so data and integration intensive, the tasks and processes can be complex and become 80 percent of the project.

INITIATING

Initiating a project, using PMI vernacular, is the beginning of what we would do to start a project. In our case, we are going to compare and use the PMI framework for our MDM project. Our assumption is that we are managing this endeavor. The PMI initiating process (for the project manager) would include the following:

1. Select and assign the project manager—I guess that's us!
2. Review the company culture, existing systems, existing processes, existing procedure, and any historical information that may benefit this project. It's extremely important to understand how past projects or similar projects were addressed and implemented in this corporation. For example, has this company ever tried to create master data before? Has it previously gathered business requirements? Were there technical specifications created? You can also review these:

    o Timelines

    o Resources

       o Knowledge areas

       o Outputs and final product

       o Other project managers who led projects

       o Stakeholder management strategies

       o How project planning and implementation was completed at this organization

3. Understand or create the business case for the MDM project. This will become part of the project charter (No. 7).

4. Divide the project into phases, such as justify, plan, analyze, design, build, and deploy.

5. Uncover initial requirements and risks. (This is high level.)

6. Start creating measurable objectives at a high level.

7. Develop a project charter. This should include the business case (step 3), the project sponsor(s), the current state of master data, the target state of master data, any alternatives, a high-level proposed solution, high-level deliverables, any budget requirements, resources required for the project, high-level risks, and a high-level project plan using the phases in step 4.

8. Identify the stakeholders. This isn't as easy as it sounds. You must consider stakeholders in departments that may be affected, but not involved, in the MDM project.

9. Develop the stakeholder management strategy. This involves creating a stakeholder register that includes information about each stakeholder (name, title, department, supervisor, contact information, major requirements, main expectations, influence on MDM project, role(s) on the project, responsibilities for the project, and any other information required to complete this project.

There's lots of work in initiating an MDM project!

PLANNING

The planning process for PMI consists of those processes that need to take place for the project manager to plan how to manage the project. The first step is determining how to plan. On my last project, I don't think we planned how to plan. We jumped in feet first, which may have been a crucial omission. Other steps include:

- Finalize requirements, and complete the scope for the project. In our example of an MDM project, our scope document would be completed during this process.
- Determine any purchases and the team that must be formed based on the requirements and the scope.
- Create a work breakdown structure and the accompanying dictionary. If you're not familiar with this, it's the high-level processes that take place, such as identifying and documenting source systems.
- Create an activity list and a network diagram.
- Estimate the resource requirements, time, and cost for the MDM project.
- Determine the critical path, and develop the schedule and the budget.
- Determine the quality standards for the product you're creating, and address what metrics can be monitored for the MDM project (number of customers, number of products, and so on).
- Plan how to communicate the project to management. This is a critical step and must be addressed in the MDM project. PMI recommends creating a stakeholder registry with information on how to communicate with them.
- Perform risk identification and risk analysis (qualitative and quantitative), with a response plan. For our MDM project, we may create a risk mitigation document.
- Prepare any procurement documents.
- Develop and finalize a project management plan and performance measurement baseline that are realistic.
- Gain formal approval of the plan, usually in the form of a sign-off. My preference is to deliver the information about the project to the sponsor and stakeholders for their approval.
- Hold a kickoff meeting to include all the team members, stakeholders, and sponsors to officially start the MDM project.

EXECUTING

You know as well as I do that 80 percent of an MDM project is design and development. Because of that, in the PMI executing process, the project manager is really managing the project—not doing the work. The work would include data modeling, metadata strategies/implementation, data profiling/quality, ETL development, and implementation. Execution includes the following:

- Perform the work based on the project manage plan. This was created in the planning process.

> There has to be a process to handle change, and the sponsor must understand the changes.

- Manage the change requests, and implement only approved changes. I chose to create an enhancement list and only implement changes that were required for the quality of the product/project. In any case, there has to be a process to handle change, and the sponsor must understand the changes.
- Make sure there is a common understanding of the project with the sponsor, the stakeholders, and the team.
- Perform quality assurance and quality audits. For the MDM project, this includes validating the data as it is retrieved from the source systems. Data profiling tools and data quality tools would be useful for our project.
- Acquire the final team. Actually, you'd better know when you need certain resources for the duration of this project. The hope is to keep continuity in the team.
- Continually evaluate project and team performance, and communicate the results as required by the sponsor and stakeholders.
- Hold team-building activities. I'm assuming this must be a few beers on Thursday evenings after work, because we have a strict schedule to meet with our MDM project.
- Use issue logs, and facilitate conflict resolution within the team, sponsors, and stakeholders.
- Send and receive information, and hold meetings where required.

This is still quite a bit of work for the project manager during a busy time. Actually, I think the project manager's job may be to keep everyone else out of the way during execution.

MONITORING AND CONTROLLING

Monitoring and controlling refers to the day-to-day activities that the project manager must handle to keep the MDM project on schedule and within budget. These activities include a tremendous amount of measuring, remeasuring, and forecasting. I've never had the luxury of working with a project manager who completed these activities for a project. Most of the MDM projects I've worked on have included multiple, short phases to deliver some value to the customer in a timely manner. A great project manager includes the following in monitoring and controlling:

- Take action to control the project; truthfully, the project manager should be in control at all times.
- Measure performance against the performance baseline. This continued measurement is a gauge for whether you're still on schedule.
- Use the metrics defined in the planning stage, and determine performance based on those metrics. Follow them over time during the project, and determine any variances in the schedule or budget.
- Influence the factors that cause changes (always be involved), and request changes that are required to create the MDM implementation.
- Perform change control, approve or reject changes, and inform stakeholders of approved changes (all based on the planning process).
- Create forecasts based on metrics.
- Gain acceptance of the deliverables of the MDM project. That includes the data and interfaces.
- Perform MDM quality control and risk audits, and report on the MDM project performance.
- Manage the budget (where required) and administer the procurements. This includes the purchase of hardware, software, and peopleware (read: human resources such as employees and contractors).

All these tasks assume that the project manager has the authority to perform them.

CLOSING

The PMI closing process includes activities that most of us have used at the end of a project. PMI assumes that a project will span more than three months. So, our MDM project would have multiple phases of three months or so, based on what master data is being integrated. Integration would also include the interfaces to (and from) other application systems across the enterprise. So closing a project includes the following:

- Confirm that the work is completed according to the requirements. I like to review the project charter, scope document, and requirements documents against what was delivered and assess whether all work was completed.
- Close any procurement activities that are still outstanding. This includes making sure all vendors get paid.
- Obtain a formal acceptance of the delivered product. In our MDM project, that would be the data. The data is updated where appropriate, and the interfaces have been tested thoroughly.
- Create a final performance report. This would include performance based on the MDM metrics, a final budget, and a schedule. This tells whether the project is on time and under budget.
- Index and store all records for this project in the knowledgebase. A lot of companies do have a great product for storing all these documents. Documents include reports, a project plan, all communications, an issues log, and more.
- Create lessons learned with the team, inform the sponsor and stakeholders, and store the lessons with other documents.
- Hand off the completed project. In our case, that would be operations and those departments responsible for the day-to-day activities of how the master data is used for the corporation.
- Release the resources. This is actually the last thing you do on any project. However, if there are other phases of the MDM initiative, you may want to consider keeping some of these people (especially the ones who know the tools and programs).

Idea 74: A Master Data Dilemma
David Loshin

In my book on MDM, I suggested a description or definition for master data as the "core business objects used in the different applications across the organization, along with their associated metadata, attributes, definitions, roles, connections, and taxonomies." I often use this definition in presentations; then I go on to provide some examples: customers, suppliers, parts, products, locations, and contact mechanisms.

At the same time, however, I've suggested that although proposing a concept as a master data domain may seem straightforward, solidifying the true specification and defining a master model might involve a little more sophistication.

> Although proposing a concept as a master data domain may seem straightforward, solidifying the true specification and defining a master model might involve a little more sophistication.

I can quickly describe a potential paradox: our presumption of a "master" repository implies that for each unique real-world entity, there can be one and only one representation in the repository. In turn, that representation contains at least those data attributes required to uniquely distinguish any entity from every other entity, and that must include all identifying attributes and their corresponding values. This means that for the customer domain, there is a record containing the identifying attributes for a customer; for an employee, there is a record containing the identifying attributes for an employee. So what happens when an employee is also a customer?

At the simplest level, it means that the values for the identifying attributes for that employee-customer exist in both the employee master and the customer master. Here is the dilemma, though: in that scenario, you end up with two records in your master database for the same entity. And this violates our presumption that for each real-world entity, there is one and only one representation in the repository.

Idea 75: Are You Building Bridges or Digging Moats?
Jim Harris

Medieval castles had moats to fortify their position, to protect themselves from outside aggressors, and to protect "us" on the inside from "them" on the outside. A moat was an important safety feature, but there still needed to be a way to get in and out of the castle. That's why draw bridges were built that could be lowered for access and raised for safety.

Different business units within an organization can sometimes resemble different fiefdoms within the same kingdom, or at other times resemble different kingdoms altogether.

What does an organization keep within the walls of its many castles?

- Data, within its data silos
- Knowledge, about its business processes and best practices
- Resources, either the allocated funding to different business units or the hoarding of the best people and technology

How much access does the rest of the organization get? Are others storming your castle, or are they too busy fortifying the defenses of their own castles?

One of my favorite topics is collaboration, because people working together is the most important success factor in any enterprise initiative. Yes, technology is a great enabler. And yes, methodology is a great guide. But neither technology nor methodology will get you very far without people working together. We all know this to be true, but knowing and doing are two very different things.

There are many perceived human divides within the enterprise. Some are created by the organizational chart ("I work for IT; you work for the business"). Others are created by geography ("I work in the Boston office; you work in the London office"). But if collaboration is so important, what are you doing to connect yourself to the rest of the organization?

work in the London office"). But if collaboration is so important, what are you doing to connect yourself to the rest of the organization? What are you doing to connect your castle to other castles? Are you building bridges or digging moats? In other words, are you trying to enable collaboration or encourage separation?

Idea 76: Making a Mess of MDM
Joyce Norris-Montanari

I recently read an *Information Management* article by my friend William McKnight called "10 Ways to Screw Up Your MDM Implementation."[vi] I think there may be more than 10 ways to screw up your MDM implementation, but William hits on some big ones like these:

1. Ignoring Agile development principles
2. Waiting until the last minute to look at your hardware needs
3. Waiting until it's time to start user acceptance testing to define the process and the participants
4. Neglecting to involve security
5. Failing to build and execute test plans
6. Keeping business governance out of the program
7. Being unprepared for organization change
8. Staffing the team solely with technicians
9. Assuming that once MDM is placed in production, it won't need patches and enhancements
10. Failing to include consultants who have led other organizations to MDM success

Sounds familiar to me! The article talks about some real issues that we see out in the trenches. For example, I met with a prospect who thought about master data after the scope for the data warehouse was completed. It caused a tremendous amount of anguish for the business users, because the requirements for master data didn't include a historical perspective. That's why a consultant would be handy for an MDM implementation.

> A stakeholders list created by the project manager, with roles and responsibilities, would be a great addition.

I have some additional thoughts:

- A stakeholders list created by the project manager, with roles and responsibilities, would be a great addition. It should be signed off on by the project sponsor, and all stakeholders should be included in the appropriate meetings.
- Requirements for the Agile approach and implementation of MDM would be helpful. They could include a strategy for the end vision (even though the vision doesn't end).
- Adding a project manager to help the consultant would be a good idea.

Idea 77: We're Saving Lives Here! MDM in Health Care
Jill Dyché

Sharon Smith was one of Baseline Consulting's first employees back in the early 1990s, and a world-class data architect. Sharon was a pro, not only at modeling complex data but facilitating often-heated data design sessions. She'd diffuse arguments by wryly exclaiming, "C'mon guys, we're not saving lives here!"

But with the rise of MDM, we might well be. As health care providers and insurers have begun implementing electronic medical records (EMRs), there has been a groundswell of interest in the Enterprise Master Patient Index (EMPI), the "single version of the truth" about individual patients across the continuum of care. Indeed, the automated reconciliation and integration of patient records had become a hot topic for health care providers.

> With the rise of MDM, we might well be saving lives.

The Bush administration's decision to establish an Office of the National Coordinator for Health Information Technology within the Department of Health and Human Services fanned the flames.

It's a complex task. Patient records, traditionally paper based, are now being digitized by the millions. EMRs by themselves, however, don't guarantee improvement. Neither does loading them onto a data warehouse, where their integrity is directly proportional to the quality of the business rules that are often hard-coded into ETL routines.

Add to that the fact that health care providers and insurers often face hundreds of competing sources for patient data. One provider we work with obtains data from dozens of hospitals, doctors' offices, pharmacies, senior care centers, and rehab clinics, not to mention unstructured data in clinicians' notes and admissions logs. The rules for correlating disparate records of a single patient can be mind-boggling.

MDM in health care should involve the automation of these rules via purpose-built hub technologies that include algorithmic rigor to recognize individual patients, eliminate conflicting data between records, and enrich those records with the appropriate and valuable data. Anything less is an intellectual exercise that won't change behaviors, drive patient personalization, or improve the quality of care. (Note to database designers: conformed dimensions aren't enough.) Reconciling that data in a sustained and formalized way, with patient master data deployed via MDM technologies, is what will save lives.

Idea 78: Entity Identification and Name Matching
David Loshin

Much of the development for data quality and MDM has centered on parties—individuals or organizations, classified in a variety of ways (such as customer, employee, agent, and partner). Many of the tools have been developed around a cult of name-matching: algorithms for parsing, standardizing, and normalizing name strings and subsidiary identifying attributes (such as location, contact mechanisms, physical characteristics, or assigned identifiers such as national identification numbers), whose similarities are compared, scored, weighted, and then factored into a decision process to (hopefully) determine that two records refer to the same real-world party.

There is a rich body of research on name-matching and a number of pretty good books. I recently met Tom Herzog, one of the authors of a book called *Data Quality and Record Linkage Techniques.* We briefly chatted about the challenges of name-matching as part of record linkage. If you're interested in understanding record linkage, his book is a good resource to have.

Meanwhile, it turns out that the world of entity identification and resolution does not solely revolve

> Much of the development for data quality and MDM has centered on parties—individuals or organizations, classified in a variety of ways (such as customer, employee, agent, and partner).

around the "cult of person-ality." The growth in electronic commerce and corresponding supply chain management and straight-through processing for product purchasing and delivery has led to an equal interest in quality of product information, as well as an interest in product data quality and MDM.

Idea 79: The Hubbub About MDM Hubs
Joyce Norris-Montanari

Dictionary.com defines *hubbub* as "a chaotic din caused by a crowd of people (for example, a hubbub of laughter and shouting) or a busy or noisy situation (for example: she fought through the hubbub)." This may be where we are with MDM hubs.

People are asking questions like these:

- Which MDM hub (repository, registry, or hybrid approach) would work best in our enterprise data architecture?
- Is a transactional style of hub the same as "registry"?
- What does coexistence mean for an MDM hub?

It seems that each vendor has its own terminology for the type of hubs its products can support. But what I'm not seeing is which type of hub would work best under certain circumstances. Data architecture is the design of quality and usage of the data in the enterprise. So an MDM project is definitely part of the enterprise data architecture. In the early days of business intelligence, we continually discussed whether an organization needed a data warehouse for historical trending and an operational data store (ODS) for integrated transactional reporting. We produced assessments based on criteria and requirements articulated by the business community. The assessments also prioritized which subject areas or sets of data should be implemented first.

Here we go with MDM, down the same path of analysis.

REPOSITORY

Although the MDM hub could be defined as a "store" or "cache" of data (or metadata) and tools to manage the master data for the enterprise, there seems to be a lot of issues surrounding the MDM hub architectural implementations.

A repository type of MDM hub holds and stores all the data required to meet the needs of the applications that consume the master data.

An MDM repository works best under these conditions:

- You already have a data warehouse or ODS. In other words, the data models for "one version of the truth" have already been created, or the enterprise is willing to create the rules and data models to support this approach.
- You have already created a "corporate" or "standard" understanding of the data elements that make up the master data. (See the previous bullet.) This requires a corporate understanding of data management and data governance.
- You have upper management buy-in, sponsorship, and participation to direct the application systems to change (if they can).

> Creating an MDM hub using a registry for linking enterprise data could be exactly what your organization needs.

- You have many source systems that must create/supply master data to the hub. These applications are also consumers of the hub data.

The worst things I see with this approach follow:

- You built it, and they did not come. In other words, you didn't get the business user or application users involved. All are stakeholders in this process.

- If you have a lot of disparate systems that create and use master data, it takes a while to design what the hub should look like.
- People try to store history in the hub, which makes it cumbersome to use. History belongs in a data warehouse.
- Creating an MDM hub-repository of data will be time-consuming but could be exactly what your organization needs. Get past all of the hubbub and get to work!

REGISTRY

An MDM registry type of hub is a metadata that supports links to important enterprise data.

An MDM registry works best under these conditions:

- Subject areas (customer, product, inventory, finance, and so on) of data do not necessarily overlap in the enterprise systems but reside in specific application systems.
- ROI is required quickly by an organization. Just install the software (after management and organization buy-in), analyze the enterprise data requirements, prioritize the effort, create the registry entries, test the entries, and adapt applications as necessary. (Make sure MDM is part of each project implemented, or you have failed.)

Registry hubs could be the perfect way to show feasibility via a prototype.

The worst things I see with this approach follow:

- The links and data from enterprise data are resynchronized. Resynchronization requires real-time updates, messaging, periodic batch processes, or night batch processes. Don't forget that you need someone to administer this environment for ongoing project implementations.
- The required enterprise data is spread across many application systems. You must consider the volume of data. Plus, you are only as fast as your slowest connection to any application for any process when using a registry type of hub.
- Tuning and administration aren't ongoing. Each new project needs to consider its contribution or usage of the MDM hub.

Creating an MDM hub using a registry for linking enterprise data could be exactly what your organization needs. Get past all the hubbub and get to work!

HYBRID

What if you started with a registry type of MDM hub and then added a repository type of MDM hub for some of the enterprise data? That's called a hybrid hub. I can see where this may be exactly what a large enterprise would implement.

Here's my understanding of what could happen:

- We needed to show ROI quickly and created a registry hub for the integration of customer data elements across three systems (financials, online customer services, marketing). The enterprise view of customer did not excessively overlap between these systems. So we created links by data element across all three systems.
- Now we need to bring in product information from five systems. Three of these systems are present due to M&A. Thus, the same product information can reside on all five systems. So we created an MDM repository hub bringing in only the best of the enterprise data across the five systems.

An MDM hybrid approach works best under these conditions:

- We start small and grow bigger.
- The environment dictates that we consider both a repository and a registry for MDM.

The worst things I see with this approach follow:

- It's necessary to manage and administer the MDM environment as an enterprise data asset.
- Ongoing maintenance and relevance analysis must be completed on a regular basis.

Creating an MDM hub using a hybrid approach to accessing enterprise data could be where your organization ends up after starting with a registry hub.

Get past all the hubbub and create MDM based on requirements and business need.

Part V:
Data Migration

Moving data from one area, system, application, or data warehouse to another can be a herculean effort. At a minimum, the process is usually rife with perils. Lamentably, most organizations vastly understate the time, money, and resources required to *successfully* move data from one area to another. The results can be disastrous, because missing, incomplete, or duplicate data can wreak havoc on basic organizational processing.

In this section, the contributors explore some of the challenges associated with this cumbersome task.

Idea 80: Planning a Data Migration? Beware of Sampling
Dylan Jones

If you want to deliver a data migration, there's one sentence that should make the hairs stand up on the back of your neck: "Let's use a sample."

The word "sample" often crops up throughout the migration project. At the start, we may decide to perform a data quality assessment on a limited sample of data.

During testing, we may decide to sample a subset of records and a limited set of attributes.

On the actual go-live day, we may approach user acceptance testing and business sign-off by testing a sample of user screens and scenarios.

The dangers of sampling are real. I once took a call from a member of Data Migration Pro who was deeply concerned that thousands of missing attributes had been found in the company's health care system several months after the migration had completed. Unfortunately, the legacy system had been decommissioned, and no archive was available. Data Migration Pro was truly up the creek without a suitable paddle.

Clearly, the company's testing had been incomplete. It should have had an archiving strategy as well, but that's a topic for another day.

Sampling is practical. If you're in the data quality rule discovery phase, you don't necessarily need to profile every record to document the data quality rules that are present. As you start to expand beyond simple data quality rules into the more complex business rules, it soon becomes apparent that sampling doesn't work. You need the complete picture to understand how the data has been manipulated over time, what

> Nowhere is sampling more dangerous than during reconciliation testing.

rules are critical and, more important, what the current health of the entire data set is.

The dangers of a sampling approach really hit home when it comes to the live migration. If your testing has been sample based, you will undoubtedly fail to create a zero defect migration, and that has to be your goal.

Many people scoff at the idea of zero defects during migration runtime, but if that isn't your goal, there's a flaw in your methodology. If you've put all the necessary project, process, and technical elements in place, you shouldn't have a single defect. Not one.

Nowhere is sampling more dangerous than during reconciliation testing, which is the process of ensuring that the data you have migrated correctly reflects the legacy environments it was extracted from. By taking a sampling approach here, you're placing your project in danger of the same problems our Data Migration Pro member experienced.

User acceptance testing, by its very nature, is sample based, so you need to augment any human testing with full data quality assessments to ensure that all the possible combinations and conditions of data following the migration have been fully validated.

There's nothing more damaging for the migration team than witnessing a successful migration in terms of zero defects at runtime but then experiencing a steady stream of complaints and dissatisfaction from the user community as data defects slowly emerge.

If you're working on a data migration right now, listen for situations in which people are taking a sampling approach, and question the validity of this practice.

Idea 81: Do You Really Know Your Business?
Dylan Jones

Do you know your business? Do you understand how it creates revenue and costs? Which customers drive the most profits? Which workers are the most efficient? Which processes create the longest lead times? How do your customers perceive what you offer?

If you don't know your business, you're missing a vital component to your data quality offering.

One of the big mistakes I used to make when starting out as a data quality practitioner was diving straight into the data. I had amassed an armory of James Bond-esque data quality gadgets and tools with a view to delivering "shock and awe" findings, highlighting defects galore in a bid to get the sponsor onside.

I wanted to focus on delivering a sense of urgency, getting the company fired up to take action. However, on many occasions in the early days, my shock and awe tactics failed to hit the mark—big time.

It was some time later that I realized I was doomed to failure:

- I hadn't fully understood the business of my client or employer.
- The client or employer hadn't fully understood his own business.

Now, the first is understandable, particularly if you're a freelancer or have been parachuted in by a consultancy to work wonders in a short time frame. But surely every business understands its own business, right?

In my experience, the answer is a resounding no; most businesses I meet don't fully understand their business, which can create a huge opportunity for the data quality practitioner.

Take these real-life situations from my past as an example of what I mean:

- A utilities company had no idea of the costs involved in doing a truck-roll to a customer site.
- A telecoms company had no idea how long it took to provision a new customer circuit.
- A charity company had no idea how many donors converted to each specific offer within the marketing campaign.
- A telecoms company had no idea who its top 10 corporate customers were by profits.

Each of these companies, and many more like them, only had a vague idea of how their business created or spent money at the detailed level.

> It's so easy to assume that customers know their business, but in my experience they don't.

In each situation, by digging deeper, asking the tough questions, and creating a 100 percent defensible financial model (that didn't exist before), I was able to carry out subsequent data quality work that enabled us to do the following:

- Identify pain points in the data that linked directly to the financial model
- Demonstrate how those pain points were affecting business measures that the company valued

- Simulate the effect of eliminating those defects (that is, sharing a vision of future performance with data quality improved

It's so easy to assume that customers know their business, but in my experience they don't—not to the level that's required for data quality improvement at any rate.

The key is to use those same data profiling and analytical skills most data quality professionals possess but point them at how the business functions instead. Analyze the data, and draw out performance measures that don't exist. Relate different data sets that have never been connected but enable you to build a clearer picture about the financial performance of the business model.

Find out how the company ticks, incorporate that with your data quality analysis, and tell the full story, not just the data story.

Idea 82: Half Measures
Phil Simon

I've written before about *Breaking Bad* (see Idea 46 on page 76), the fascinating show on AMC about a high school science teacher with an interesting side job manufacturing crystal meth. Lamentably in organizations, sometimes events and trends cause data quality to, well, break bad.

Let's revisit the show in the context of half measures, the title of one of the best episodes of the previous season. For the purposes of this Idea, half measures represent compromises made during data quality and cleanup endeavors. For example, let's say that an organization's systems contain years of suspect data. It intends to clean up what it needs, purge what it doesn't, and archive all of it in the event of an unexpected issue. Of course, things break bad in the form of delays, exceeded budgets, politics, and all other sorts of fun stuff.

Specific half measures may include these:

- Cleaning up some of the data
- Postponing parts of the data cleanup efforts
- Taking a "wait and see" approach as more issues are unearthed

So, when are half measures appropriate?

COMPLETELY APPROPRIATE

Plowing ahead with data cleanup without knowing the full range of consequences is a bad idea. To be sure, individual applications and systems have safeguards to prevent orphaned records and other undesirable outcomes. However, think about disparate systems stitched together by interfaces or other ETL tools. Consider the following questions:

- Is there general agreement on what needs to be done? What about how to do it?
- What are the downstream effects in System A of changing records in System B?
- Are we breaking anything down the road?
- Have we adequately tested this?
- Does the organization have the time and resources to do what needs to be done?

If you can't comfortably answer questions like these, half measures are entirely appropriate.

COMPLETELY INAPPROPRIATE

Half measures for the sake of half measures irritate me. Caution is fine and dandy, but sometimes organizations need to take decisive action and just plain get something done. There are windows of resource, financial, and business opportunity that come along once in a while.

Half measures are inappropriate in the following situations:

- Key parties cannot reach agreement on what needs to be done—much less how to do it.
- Downstream effects have been accounted for.
- Interfaces and ETL tools have been sufficiently tested—and have passed those tests.
- The time, resources, and budget to "go the full nine" have been arranged.

> One of the tricks of management—perhaps *the* greatest trick—is to know when to wield the carrot or the stick, when to stay or go, when to expand or contract.

JUDGMENT CALLS

Of course, much lies between "completely appropriate and completely inappropriate). One of the tricks of management—perhaps the greatest trick—is to know when to wield the carrot or the stick, when to stay or go, when to expand or contract. Rarely will an organization and its end users be completely ready for change. Usually, at least a few key people will stand up and say, "We're not ready."

SIMON SAYS

Look, if large questions remain unanswered, undertaking a major data quality or cleanup initiative is hardly a wise idea. Understand that different individuals and factions in large organizations have vested interests in taking action, just as others are biased toward maintaining the status quo. This is agency theory 101. Don't wait for the "perfect" time to cleanse your data; it doesn't exist. Find a good time, and do what you can.

Idea 83: How to Escape the Data Migration Doldrums
Dylan Jones

The Doldrums: light, shifting, and sometimes completely absent winds—are notorious for trapping sailing ships for days (or even weeks) without enough wind to power their sails.—Wikipedia

Working on a data migration, particularly a large project, can often feel like you're stranded on the ocean, waiting for a favorable wind to push you forward to the go-live date.

There are generally two schools of thought for large-scale data migration projects. The first is the all-or-nothing "big bang" approach. Analyze, design, build, test (endlessly), and then move the data in one swift (you hope) operation.

The second method (my preference, as much for the sake of personal sanity) is the Agile approach. Deliver smaller "business-focused chunks" of data that get the new target system into operation far quicker. This approach requires a lot more thought around transitioning customers, users, and data in complete harmony, but it is undoubtedly the best way to get out of the data migration doldrums.

The problem with the data migration doldrums is that there is no apparent movement in the project. There's nothing tangible to show for your labor except the steady slog of cleaning up data, building out rules, and progressive baldness as you pull your hair out after every target system design change is announced, resulting in an overhaul of your migration rules, once again.

> You must try your utmost to avoid the long, drawn-out big bang and do everything in your power to deliver earlier, faster, and more frequently.

In one migration I was involved with, the project dragged on for so long the business actually changed its mind—twice—over which legacy systems, subject areas, and even target systems would be required. To escape the data migration doldrums, there has to be one word stamped on the head of every participant in the project: delivery. You must try your utmost to avoid the long, drawn-out big bang and do everything in your power to deliver earlier, faster, and more frequently.

Big bang is still common, but the death knell is sounding. The next time you witness a huge waterfall project plan leading up to the physical migration, question the logic of this approach and see how you can create cycles of delivery, each one creating tangible value. Often, I find that the reasons these questions aren't asked stems from the fact that, "That's not the way we normally do it around here." There are often no practical reasons why an iterative, doldrum-busting approach won't work.

Idea 84: Data Migration Myths and Legends
Dylan Jones

I don't get it. We moved an entire data center in three weeks last year, and now you're telling me I have to pay for all of these analysis activities that will take three months, minimum?

The preceding quote was from a particularly irate senior manager who had grown frustrated at my continued demand to undertake a thorough data discovery and data quality assessment prior to the largest migration her business unit had ever undertaken. The problems stemmed from her perception of what data migration should involve, and here I was trying to shatter her dream of a rapid build and go-live. I felt like the data migration Grinch.

Data migration has many myths and legends that can seriously undermine your ability to put in place anything resembling best practice. It's important to get them all out into the open so you can help reshape misconceptions. It's often fear and lack of awareness that are the causes of migration failure, not necessarily some technical mishap or poor planning.

Senior management can often assume that what you're demanding is too extreme for their data—"Our data is about 90 percent correct; why do we need data quality?" When budgets start getting tight, managers can trim back the essentials with a view to "getting started" and "getting some data moving."

Of course, you have to fully understand the pressures that senior management are facing. With a new target system looming, no one wants his team to be holding up the wondrous gifts the target system will deliver to the business.

What are some of the common myths and legends of data migration so we can listen for them and ensure we get into myth-busting mode?

MYTH 1: DATA MIGRATION IS A "TECHIE PROJECT"

Data belongs to IT, right?

A lot of data migration projects are still driven far too much by technical activities and lack sufficient business engagement. The data quality management element of a data migration is a classic example. Often seen as an activity of "cleansing," the business can scarcely be seen. In fact, the correct approach is to integrate the business into the core of your data quality processes so that they call the shots on prioritization and resolution.

MYTH 2: DATA MIGRATION IS ABOUT MOVING DATA

Data migration obviously moves data between legacy and target environments, but this is a simplistic view that misses the big picture. We're transitioning a business and all the complexity that goes with that. By focusing solely on the data, we can forget that our migration activities must align with decommissioning, training and education, stakeholder management, new business services, and functions.

MYTH 3: DATA MIGRATION IS A SERIES OF TASKS ON THE SYSTEM IMPLEMENTATION PROJECT PLAN

Quite often migration projects are bundled in with the system implementation because it appears to make sense. They both have similar objectives, after all. Data migration should always be treated as a distinct project because the skills, technologies, and tactics are quite distinct to other projects. It's obviously critical to align your objectives and deliverables with the wider program, but bundling all your activities into one grand project puts you on the fast-track to data migration failure.

MYTH 4: IF THE DATA IS GOOD ENOUGH IN LEGACY, IT WILL BE GOOD ENOUGH IN THE TARGET

This myth has been passed down from generation to generation and is a favorite with the business sponsor who panics at the sight of those data quality estimates.

We're running a business perfectly well on the data we've got; let's get it into the target and clean up there.

The problem is that your new system is not the same. No matter how closely you try to model the existing functions in the new world system, there will be differences. These differences will place pressure on the data to perform functions it was never designed for.

> To make your data migration successful, you have to put some serious skin in the game.

In one engagement, a client wished to collapse 17 systems into one state-of-the-art asset management system that could pinpoint equipment to within a few inches within any building. Unfortunately, the client hadn't reckoned on 10 years of engineers typing in freehand text to describe the current equipment locations. The data was accurate, complete, and trusted in the legacy environment, but ill prepared for the brave new world that beckoned.

MYTH 5: WE CAN JUST OUTSOURCE EVERYTHING AND MAKE THE PROBLEM GO AWAY

Closely related to myth 1 is the myth that if we pay large enough sums of money, someone will take this data migration hot potato off our hands.

The reality is that to make your data migration successful, you have to put some serious skin in the game. The most able internal developers, architects, analysts, and business leads have to be taken out of their present roles and made to commit their expertise to the project.

Sponsors have to contribute to data quality review sessions and take far more of a role than simply signing off milestones they have absolutely no understanding of. You can never completely outsource a data migration and expect a perfect result. It is your data, your business, and your customers at stake. It demands your involvement to get the right outcome.

Idea 85: Mergers and Acquisitions
Rich Murnane

My shop was recently purchased by another company, which is a strange feeling indeed. Since the announcement, the message to our staff has been "business as usual," and the actions taken by our senior management certainly do, in fact, feel like nothing significant has changed. So, business as usual it is, and it's so far so good from my window of the world.

My previous shop was a hardware and electronic component distributor, and we were always the ones doing the buying. During my tenure, we seemed to acquire at least one other distributor each year, and it was quite fun to be part of. Upon announcement of the M&A, the teams would do a technology audit of the shop we were buying; we data geeks were always interested in grabbing all types of data from the shop this way. Once we had a handle on where the company's data (such as customer, product, and sales data) was stored, we began working with the staff to pull the data out of those systems and start the integration projects on our side. Rarely did the shop being purchased have "single sources of the truth" for its primary types of data; most times we'd end up having to pull extracts from "this" system and "that" system and figure out what to do with the data.

> Matching was always the most fun and challenging part of these M&A projects.

STEP 1: PROFILING

Once we received extracts from these source systems, our next step was to understand the data we received. To do this, we profiled the records and checked to see if the results of the profiling were in line with whatever documentation we received with the data. Many times we thought we were going to get one thing and ended up with something else. You have to remember that typically the staff of the other shop was still trying to keep its company running while satisfying all our requests, all while trying to figure out what's going on with their jobs. It wasn't much fun for them, so we had to be patient.

STEP 2: CLEANSING

After profiling and discovering things about the company's data, the next step involved standardizing the data as best we could. We'd also try to remove any duplicate records and records that weren't needed (test records, records for customers who never had orders, and so on). Removing duplicate records was even more important when we were merging more than one extract.

STEP 3: MATCHING

Once we cleaned up the data we received, we'd try to match the company's data to ours. This was always the most fun and challenging part of these M&A projects. Once we'd performed initial matches, we'd communicate our match rates to the M&A project managers. The project managers always pushed us to see what we could do better for our matching. Looking back now, I'm sure there were some cool technologies I could have used, but at the time we weren't doing any "black magic."

STEP 4: MERGING

Merging the company's data with ours was typically pretty straightforward because we'd already done the matching. Before coding, we'd meet with our different business units and ask them "what if" questions, such as, "What if their data has records ours does not?" and "What if their data matches ours, but some fields are different?" and "They have this really cool piece of data that we don't have—can we integrate that, too?" Once we had the business rules ironed out, we'd design, code, and test the ETL code. Each insert and update on our data was tracked and reported on so we could report results to our managers as well as have an audit trail—just in case.

LAST STEPS: TESTING AND COMMUNICATION

I can't say enough about testing. M&A projects are usually completed in a fast and furious manner, and often people neglect to test the results. But omitting this step from your project can be disastrous. After we were comfortable with our test results, we thoroughly communicated the results to our M&A project managers and other senior management. Simple metrics such as Customer Count and Product Count before and after are what these folks needed to know.

If it sounds like I'm oversimplifying the process, I am; there are too many facets of an M&A to write about in one short Idea. If you're a data geek who's going to be involved in your first M&A project, you're in for a wild ride. Buckle your seat belt and hold on tight!

Idea 86: How to Orchestrate a Data Migration Failure
Dylan Jones

Let's talk a little about how the decisions we make right at the outset of a data migration project will spell success or failure down the line. (Okay, that's a nice way of saying this is really a rant about companies that drive me insane by refusing to allow common sense onto their data migration projects).

Although we may read that data migration projects frequently fail at the implementation phase, a recent personal example illustrates how most projects are doomed even before the project is initiated.

Case in point is a project that I was introduced to a couple of years ago. I went along and met the systems integrator responsible for the entire migration.

Immediately, alarm bells were ringing based on the quantity of resources the systems integrator wanted to hire to deliver the project. The company had just won the project days before and was frantically trying to resource a huge team to hit the ground running. This worried me.

Yes, it's common practice to bolster your troops, particularly when some specialist domain knowledge or technical expertise may be lacking. But if your systems integrator has to recruit 90 percent of its project team on the open market, there are always going to be problems integrating such a fresh and untested resource.

If you're a client who has hired a systems integrator who immediately starts looking for skills to deliver the project, this should be a warning sign to you.

The second issue I witnessed was a lack of expert data migration domain knowledge. It was nonexistent. After pointing out that the company really needed an expert in complex data migration projects to define the strategy and structure of the team (among many other tasks), I was told privately that the company was struggling to balance the books while publicly the excuse was that the end client "had already defined the migration strategy, so a data migration domain expert was no longer necessary." The client strategy consisted of, "Please migrate our systems on this date. Thank you."

If you're a data migration client with a systems integrator who does not have an extremely experienced data migration expert onboard, this should be a warning to you.

Perhaps the biggest issue lay in the timing and roadmap. I was shown a project delivery roadmap that highlighted the various milestones. There was a requirement to migrate hundreds of systems in less than two years. I did a rough calculation on a piece of paper showing that, with the team size proposed, roughly 2–3 people would have to complete a migration something like every 1–2 weeks—all this with a completely unproven team, with no migra-

> The real failure is a human one, and ultimately it is our old adversary, common sense, that is to blame.

tion domain expert, and with no migration technology platform in place. I mentioned the need for data discovery and a data quality platform, and "What's that?" was the reply I received.

With the first migration scheduled for completion within a few weeks, I pointed out that the company had orchestrated a 100 percent failure; there could be no other outcome. Everyone I spoke with who was hired or consulted by the systems integrator agreed: the project was unfeasible.

Yet the project went ahead despite every person who had any data migration experience openly acknowledging it would fail.

If you're a client that sets the roadmap solely based on commercial or regulatory requirements, but the systems integrator fails to challenge or validate your assumptions, this should be a warning sign to you.

So where are we today?

Well, the reason for this Idea is that I recently met one of the project members who privately admitted that the project was not in the best of shapes. Deliverables were slipping, and the systems integrator was struggling, to put it mildly.

At this point I suspect there is a great deal of arm-waving, panic resourcing, and endless rescoping exercises, but it is probably too late. The decisions that led to this failure were made well before the project started.

Ultimately, I'm sure we'll hear of the technical challenges this project presented and a whole other rack of reasons, but the real failure is a human one, and ultimately it is our old adversary, common sense, that is to blame.

If you're prepared to put the fate of your entire business strategy in one untried, untested company and then absolve yourself of posing the most obvious of questions, sadly, the statistics for data migration are only going to rise.

Idea 87: The HedgeFoxian Hypothesis
Jim Harris

Data quality, MDM, and data governance are terms to describe enterprise initiatives. Lively debates can be had over whether these terms are related or if one is the primary discipline and the others are subordinates. Regardless, many organizations look for a framework to follow, either "one theory to rule them all" or a one-size-fits-all methodology. Is it better to approach such a complex challenge with one all-encompassing "theory of everything" or with a best practice based on awareness and adaptation?

THE HEDGEHOG AND THE FOX

In his excellent essay "The Hedgehog and the Fox," Isaiah Berlin described two different types of thinkers using the ancient Greek expression:

The Fox knows many things, but the Hedgehog knows one big thing.

The particular choice of animals was not random. The hedgehog is a small animal covered with spines. When attacked, its only defense is to roll itself into a ball so that all of its spines point outward and in every direction. The fox resembles a small dog. Both its defense and attack are based

> Is it better to approach such a complex challenge with one all-encompassing "theory of everything" or with a best practice based on awareness and adaptation?

on its cunning adaptation to the present situation. It's also one of the hedgehog's few predators.

Extending the analogy used in Berlin's essay, let's take a closer look at the characteristics of the Hedgehog and the Fox in relation to enterprise initiatives.

THE HEDGEHOG

The Hedgehog views the world through the lens of a single all-encompassing theory, thriving on the certainty and control that comes from "just following the plan."

The plan provides authority—usually dictated by a renowned specialist. The Hedgehog doesn't like to think too much; it simply wants to learn—and then obey—the rules. Despite the all-encompassing nature of the Hedgehog's worldview, it tends to be easily criticized for oversimplifying complex challenges.

However, as William of Ockham famously wrote:

Entia non sunt multiplicanda praeter necessitatem.

If your Latin is a little rusty, that phrase (also known as Ockham's razor) translates directly as, "Entities must not be multiplied beyond necessity," or far more commonly as, "The simplest answer is usually the correct answer," and even more colloquially as, "Keep it simple, stupid."

Our general disdain of complexity often leads to our general preference for simplicity. When simplicity combines with idealism, it becomes a powerful motivation. And imagining an idyllic future without any of the current limitations or obstacles that prevent optimal business performance is a difficult vision to resist. The Hedgehog becomes hyper-focused on this vision of a better tomorrow and its promise of finally bringing order to today's seemingly endless chaos.

The fatal flaw of the Hedgehog is its blind persistence. When complexity is encountered, it is either conveniently ignored or dismissed as irrelevant in the "grand scheme of things." Hedgehogs can make seemingly impressive progress for a long period of time, but without actually achieving anything because their ultimate goal was never attainable.

When the Hedgehog fails, it simply assumes that the wrong theory was selected, or it substitutes a packaged solution from a software vendor, replacing a belief in following "the right methodology" with a belief in implementing "the right technology." Either way, a new grand theory or magical technology is sought and easily found, and then history slowly and expensively repeats itself.

THE FOX

The Fox views the world through the kaleidoscope of a variety of experiences, thriving on doubt and chaos and knowing that the only constant is change. The Fox doesn't believe in a one-size-fits-all solution—even for a simple problem—and knows an enterprise initiative is fraught with both complexities and the unexpected.

Skeptical of authority and specialists, the Fox is a generalist, jack of all trades, master of none, but master of integrating disparate disciplines into practical solutions. The Fox becomes hyper-active—goes with the flow, tries to build and sustain momentum, and is always looking to make adjustments whenever necessary.

The fatal flaw of the Fox is its need for independence and autonomy. The Fox is not a pack animal and often believes it is best to be an army of one. Therefore, the Fox typically resists collaboration—especially with other Foxes.

When the Fox fails, it tends to just move on to the next challenge, preferably one where everyone else gets out of its way and lets it do whatever has to be done.

THE HEDGEHOG OR THE FOX?

The simplicity and idealism of the Hedgehog is certainly admirable—as is the cunning and adaptability of the Fox. When embarking on an enterprise initiative, is it better to be the Hedgehog or the Fox?

The Hedgehog wants to be told what to do. The Fox wants to figure it out on its own.

The Hedgehog thrives in a environment where every action can be carefully planned in advance—and by someone else. The Fox thrives in an environment where every action is executed in the moment—responding to what it believes is necessary right now.

Starting and running an enterprise initiative like the Hedgehog doesn't work. But starting and running an enterprise initiative like the Fox doesn't work either.

So if neither an "all Hedgehog" nor an "all Fox" approach works as a viable strategy, perhaps the best qualities of each need to be combined. I refer to this idea as The HedgeFoxian Hypothesis.

THE HEDGEFOXIAN HYPOTHESIS

The Hedgehog and the Fox have much to learn from each other. What is needed is the creation of a hybrid species—the HedgeFox.

The HedgeFox:

- Understands the vision and appreciates the potential represented by the "theory of everything," but it tempers it with the realities of the current environment.
- Knows that any theory only becomes practical when its ideas can be spread—and by allowing others to customize it to fit current and future needs.
- Values both the specialist and the generalist, knowing each is necessary.
- Embraces complexity and avoids oversimplification by advocating an iterative implementation leveraging recurring iterations of relatively short duration.
- Plans like the Fox by evaluating myriad best practices and then customizing an approach for the current iteration.
- Implements like the Hedgehog, carefully following the plan for the current iteration step by step.

Each subsequent iteration repeats this best practice:

Plan like the Fox, but implement like the Hedgehog.

This allows the enterprise initiative to follow what works for as long as it works, without being afraid to adjust as necessary when circumstances inevitably change.

Idea 88: Unspoken Truths
Phil Simon

WHAT CLIENTS DON'T TELL CONSULTANTS

I was recently perusing the search terms that people used to find my own personal site and blog and came across the query, "What do clients not tell consultants?"

Perhaps 15 years ago in grad school, I wouldn't have had a sufficient answer to that question. After all, what did I know about such things? Well, things change. Hardened by nearly as many years in the corporate and technology worlds, however, I have no shortage of opinions.

Left Unsaid

Like many consultants, I often have been left holding the bag on data conversion and migration projects. Consider a recent project in which an organization brought me in late to a project with an intractable go-live date. I essentially had three months to convert essential employee data from a series of legacy systems into the new applications. Sound aggressive? Oh, it gets better.

The data was, quite simply, a mess. No one took ownership over data quality issues; no one could be bothered with their resolution. In other words, forget being proactive. This organization couldn't even be reactive.

To be sure, this project was atypical with respect to its level of dysfunction. Nevertheless, there were certainly parallels between this one and many of the projects on which I have worked. In other words, more often than not, organizations fail to tell me about the following:

- The quality of their legacy data
- The completeness of their legacy data

- The number of sources of legacy data (including all standalone databases, spreadsheets, paper files, and other homegrown apps)
- The results of previous attempts to cleanse data
- Institutional or cultural roadblocks
- People issues related to these issues

Now, sometimes this withholding is intentional, and sometimes the people involved just don't know. As a seasoned consultant, of course, I know enough to ask these questions before even accepting the gig. Of course, it's not as if I can administer a polygraph test. Ultimately, I have to make an educated decision about whether the assignment is worth taking.

Determining Responsibility and the Consequences of Keeping Quiet

All of this begs the following questions:

- Does a client have to tell its consultants everything?
- If everything is divulged, is the client absolved from blame if and when things go astray?

The answers, of course, are "no." However, think for a moment about the consequences of failing to divulge critical pieces of information:

- Deadlines may be missed.
- Estimates on project cost may well fall by the wayside.
- Critical functionality might have to be cut to satisfy a key date.
- Issues may not be identified or addressed in a timely manner.

Considering all the above, doesn't it benefit clients to air their dirty laundry to consultants as soon as possible? How can consultants be partners when they don't know all the facts?

WHAT CONSULTANTS DON'T TELL CLIENTS

Now it's time to turn the table. But, before I do, a few disclaimers are in order.

At least two-thirds of my annual income comes from consulting, and this has been the case for nearly 10 years. Translation: I tend to write from the consultant's perspective. Do with that what you will.

I'm going to include the salespeople here from system integrators (SIs) and consultancies. Although they're not consultants per se, most clients justifiably do not draw the distinction between these two groups when data migration and integration projects run amok.

I'm not inherently biased against salespeople, a topic that I recently addressed in an interview. I've just seen certain shenanigans more than once before on the sales' side.

I'm obviously writing here on general terms and from my own perspective. If you're a consultant or salesperson, you may be reading this and thinking, "I would never nor have never done that." I believe you.

Unaddressed Questions

In any economy (much less a challenging one), SIs have an incentive to overlook potentially show-stopping data and people issues when, quite frankly, they ought to know better. This may take one of several forms:

- Failing to ask key questions during the sales cycle. How old is the data? Has the data ever been profiled?
- Determining the sources of information that need to be cleansed and ultimately loaded into the new system or application.
- Opting to overlook answers to these questions that will probably inflate the cost of the engagement and risk not getting the deal.
- Inappropriately tweaking estimates to lower immediate costs, knowing full well that the SI will submit change requests later in the project once the client's checks have cleared.

Now, when a project goes awry and things get contentious, it's simply wrong to instinctively blame the consultants and salespeople. Although circumstances vary, in many cases, there's simply no way for the SI to have known the severity of the data and people challenges at any particular client. No project estimating tool can accurately account for the cauldron of issues endemic at many dysfunctional organizations. It's unreasonable to expect an SI to send in a team of consultants to do weeks' worth of data profiling and chalk the costs up as "pre-sales."

Simon Says: Advice for Clients Evaluating Consultancies

For clients interviewing prospective implementation partners, understand that even estimates with the best intentions are just that: estimates. Depending on the way the contract is ultimately structured (travel and expense versus fixed bid), expect your new partners to behave accordingly. If the client opts for the former, all issues will probably be addressed and hopefully resolved—on the client's dime. On fixed-bid projects, consultants are incentivized to complete the work as quickly as possible and move to the next client. Understand this going in, and make decisions about error resolution accordingly. There is such a thing as tomorrow, especially regarding nonessential data.

> Be realistic and transparent.

Be realistic and transparent. CIOs and their teams should not expect consultants to be clairvoyant with respect to data issues. Nor are consultants miracle workers. Clients should know that SIs have their own predispositions—just like they themselves do. Don't hide key problems for the purposes of securing the best overall project bid. You're looking for a partner, not a scapegoat or a punching bag.

Be realistic and transparent.

WHAT CLIENTS DON'T TELL EACH OTHER

Okay, enough talk about consultants. Now it's time to cover that which clients don't tell each other.

A Definition and Disclaimers

Before continuing, I want to be clear here about what I mean by "clients." I'm talking about end users from different lines of business. HR, marketing, and finance folks qualify. I'm specifically excluding IT folks here because, although they technically may be clients, they should not be the ones making decisions about how enterprise data is converted. Of course, this often happens, but that's a discussion over beers one day…

Also, allow me to state my typical disclaimers:

- I used to work on the client side before becoming a consultant. Obviously, I still interact with clients on a regular basis.
- These are generalizations based on my years of professional experience. They may not apply to you and your organization.

DANGEROUS MIND-SETS

Let's run through a hypothetical example. During the sales cycle, different software vendors and system integrators compete for Client X's business. Each will position itself as uniquely qualified to serve X's needs. Each will claim that it offers the most flexibility, most knowledgeable resources, lowest total cost of ownership (TCO), and so on. All this is fine and dandy, but the focus at Client

X tends to be external, placed on what the vendors and SIs can do for X, not what X end users need to do for each other for the project to be successful.

Good consultants (and I like to put myself in this category) emphasize not simply what clients need to do during a system or data migration project. While delicate during the sales cycle among often apprehensive clients, we attempt to identify what clients won't do, for both consultant and for each other—or at least don't want to do. We try to manifest the unspoken assumptions and mentalities that can doom a project from day one.

Now, let's look at four major examples of these pernicious assumptions and mentalities. Although I've written them in the first person, often people use much more creative (and, I'd argue, less honest) expressions that essentially hit the same mark.

I Like My Data, Not Yours

I once saw a major ERP initiative stall over attempts to get everyone to use the same core HR data elements, such as job codes. One VP hemmed and hawed about bogus reasons not to use the global lists, but fundamentally he liked his data more than the standardized data set. The IT lead for the global project expressed his frustration to me because of certain VPs' unwillingness to get with the program.

It Shouldn't Be My Responsibility to Clean Up Historical Data

In one project a few years ago, end users firmly expected internal IT personnel to not only provide data irregularities and issues to investigate, but the "correct" answers as well. Astonishing. This raises the questions:

- If IT is identifying and resolving data issues, what is the role of the line manager?
- Does IT really possess the expertise to diagnose complicated payroll and billing issues?

I Don't Know How to Properly Configure the New System; Tell Me

This one is priceless, and I swear I'm not making it up. On a recent project, I was loading employee data and, because of some system configuration issues, paychecks were "off." When I pointed out that the issue stemmed from a particular local tax not being activated in the new system (something easily done), an end user asked me, "Well, do we need that?"

Innocuous question, to be sure. But the translation is shocking:

I have no idea if we've been doing things correctly for as long as I've been here. Although I could look it up or ask the appropriate personnel, it's easier for me to blame you if you're wrong. What's the correct setup?

Auditors would have a field day with consultants coming in and dictating policy in an organization.

I'm Not Sure About How Much Historical Information Needs to Be Kept

Just about every application that I've ever seen or used has tools to facilitate importing massive amounts of data, subject to business rules defined in the system. Conversion programs can load just about as many records as the database will hold. Consider the following questions:

- How much data is truly needed? (Remember that must-have and nice-to-have are two entirely different things.)
- Given that older data is typically dirtier than its more recent counterpart, do the benefits of loading absolutely everything justify their costs?
- Does anyone really care that a $17.44 invoice was paid back in 1982?

Simon Says: Try to Identify People and Data Issues as Early as Possible

Clients often misplace blame when data migration projects run amok. If I only had a nickel for every time that an end user told me, "That's not what the salesperson said."

Build assumptions into statements of work. Many clients mistakenly believe that these are only necessary for consultants and vendors to cover themselves in the event that things break bad. No. Explicitly laying out all assumptions forces client end users to understand the decisions and actions that they need to take for data migration projects to be successful.

Idea 89: Are You Playing Data Migration Jenga?
Dylan Jones

Some months ago I presented at a data migration event in the UK. While chatting with some of the attendees, it was interesting to hear the different approaches that people were taking in terms of skills, technologies, methodology, management, accountability, and systems integrator partnerships.

Many had experienced the common signs of data migration failure—blown budgets, data quality disasters, and the resulting implementation delays. One person in particular, a data migration developer, was critical of the tactics that his organization had adopted and discussed at length his approach on the organization's last migration.

> Every component of your data migration strategy has a structural role to play.

The organization had apparently started out with good intentions. After reading some best practices, it had even decided to carry out some upfront analysis and discover the danger zones before the migration itself kicked off. What followed was a classic data migration nightmare.

First, the deadline for the implementation moved forward several months due to strategic pressure. As a result, the analysis and design phases had their delivery dates brought forward. This, in turn, created a great deal of pressure on the design teams because the target architecture was still in flux, making it increasingly difficult to tie down the migration mappings and physical design.

As the analysis period was chopped, a lot of assumptions and guesswork began to creep into the project. Data quality analysis also suffered because there simply wasn't sufficient time to measure the quality of data across the entire data landscape.

The project leader, with an eye on the looming live date, urged the development team to accelerate the build phase and "get some data moving," so the team members would have a better chance of getting something across to the target in time for the live launch. Testing began to suffer; with a small team, many of the resources were being swapped endlessly, putting out fires on a daily basis.

The result was apparently chaos and a five-month delay as team members fought to resolve the many issues that came from poor planning, poor skills allocation, lack of analysis, and subsequent implementation failures.

The developer likened the experience to the game *Jenga*. The team members had initially built a strong foundation for the project, but as various components were pulled out, the core structure began to weaken and eventually collapse.

The reality with data migration is that you cannot cut corners. Every component of your data migration strategy has a structural role to play. I remember carrying out a project assessment for one company that was adamant it was "not doing data quality" because of the perceived time and effort involved. Despite my protestations, the company proceeded to lurch from delay to delay, taking far longer than anticipated.

If you do want to eliminate a core component from your data migration strategy, you simply must adopt a risk assessment. In the midst of confusion, fear, and recrimination, it's all too easy for wholesale changes to take place, but the net effect is nearly always a lengthier, more costly project; there are no get-out-of-jail cards.

Examine the risk of cutting key staff, important technology, analysis phases, or data quality management, and ask yourself some critical questions:

- Will this action deliver a better result for the customers and shareholders?
- What downstream activities will be impacted by omission of this data migration component?
- How will this affect morale?
- What is the business case for eliminating this component?
- Is the team behind me on this decision?
- Have I created an exhaustive list of pros and cons?

In nearly every migration I've been involved with, when people begin playing "Data Migration Jenga," it's typically through a position of fear, confusion, or poor understanding. Take the time to study your decision before removing those data migration Jenga blocks.

Part VI:
Metadata, Miscellany, and Final Thoughts

Data about data has never been more important, because it drives data management, quality, and governance. Organizations that haven't properly defined key fields in their applications and databases are at risk of encountering major issues down the road.

Metadata gets to the root of many data-related issues. In many large organizations, asking 10 people what they mean by *customer* is likely to provoke 10 different answers. And, without common ground on key precepts, how can an organization make optimal decisions? The short answer is that it can't.

In this section, the contributors discuss some of the issues related to metadata. In the second part of this section, they riff on a number of random data-related topics.

Idea 90: Metadata and 3-D Glasses
David Loshin

"What is the definition of 'customer'?" How many meetings (and wasted hours) have been spent attempting to answer this question? After being involved in literally hundreds of conversations regarding the never-ending process of resolving critical metadata definitions, I never tire of the opportunity to level-set about data governance, stewardship, and the metadata/harmonization albatross.

PERSPECTIVE 1

Even asking the question, "What is the definition of 'customer'?" betrays a gap in assessing information use horizontally across the organization. The fact is that the precise semantics of terms like "customer," "product," "part," and "supplier" erode as each term is used in more contexts. And because everybody already has an innate understanding of what the term means, there's no reason to be explicit about its definition. The only problem happens when stakeholder A wants to use stakeholder B's "customer" data for A's own purposes, and it turns out that they are actually talking about two completely different things, with different definitions, attributes, and quality characteristics.

PERSPECTIVE 2

Business applications are typically architected to meet functional requirements supporting transaction processing or operational activities. Analysis is an afterthought that relies on grabbing data from the operational systems. Yet the advocates for metadata are the data warehouse/business intelligence folks, grasping for some meaning onto which to hang their hats. (Okay, that's a bit of a mixed metaphor, but cut me some slack!)

PERSPECTIVE 3

What's the level of effort necessary for effective metadata management? Do a thought experiment. In your organization,

- How many applications are there?
- How many databases does each application touch?
- How many tables are in each database?
- How many attributes are in each table?
- Multiply these numbers together—that's the number of data elements to be cataloged in the metadata repository.
- How much time does it take to rationalize a data element's metadata? Let's speculate optimistically with 2 hours each.
- Multiple the number of data elements by 2, and that's the number of hours it will take to get your metadata cataloged.

PERSPECTIVE 4

When is metadata used? Despite all the expert advice about enterprise metadata and its value to the organization, we are still seeing some questions regarding its use, except for specific purposes such as developing a reporting and business intelligence program that is rationalized with the business applications.

From these perspectives, it becomes a good idea to limit the scope of your metadata activity and integrate it much earlier in the system development life cycle. By defining your data concepts before you build the databases, you simplify the associated activities (such as source-to-target mapping and data migrations).

> Instead of one customer, there are "prospective customers," "good customers," "business customers," "residential customers," "wholesale customers," and more.

But getting back to the first question about what is meant by "customer"—we'd love the ability to put on a pair of 3-D glasses and have all the different versions merge into one beautiful, rationalized definition that everyone can share. But that image is just an illusion: there's no one definition for most of the commonly used terms. More likely, there are qualified concepts that are distinct, and business processes can benefit from a differentiation and a precise definition for each.

Instead of one customer, there are "prospective customers," "good customers," "business customers," "residential customers," "wholesale customers," and more. Each has attributes that are slightly different (and relevant) to the consuming business processes. These qualifications are based on the business use, and the differentiation process reveals the common characteristics that benefit the downstream data consumers. So use those 3-D glasses in reverse: look at what you think is one concept, and try to break it out into its component (red and blue blurry) visages; then figure out why they don't all mean the same thing. That may do two things: reduce the amount of time arguing about that single definition, and create more clarity on what things really do mean.

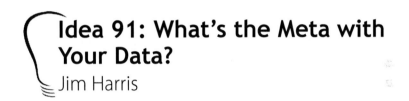

Idea 91: What's the Meta with Your Data?
Jim Harris

There are many dimensions of data quality—completeness, consistency, accuracy, and timeliness, to name just a few of the most common. However, one commonly overlooked dimension is metadata.

I know. Some of you are probably saying:

Jim, what's the matter with you? Metadata is not a dimension of data quality.

With all due respect (as always, of course!), my response is this:

Sometimes, the best way to know what's the matter with your data quality is to ask—what's the meta with your data?

THE MEANING OF METADATA

The simplest definition for metadata is "data about data." In other words, metadata can be thought of as a label that provides a definition, description, and context for data. Common examples include relational table definitions and flat file layouts. More detailed examples of metadata include conceptual and logical data models. Therefore, metadata—among its many other uses—often plays an integral role in determining your data usage.

> You should always verify the metadata as well as the data.

THE PERFECT WRONG ANSWER

As Henrik Liliendahl Sørensen recently explained on his blog,[vii] the shared understanding of the label (metadata) attached to many key business metrics can represent the real data quality issue associated with the metric. Furthermore, ignoring this important point can lead to providing the perfect wrong answer to common business questions.

YOUR WATCH TOTAL

A famous quote, sometimes referred to as Segal's Law, states that:

"A man with one watch knows what time it is. A man with two watches is never sure."

When it comes to the metrics used to make (or explain) critical business decisions, I've often witnessed the "we have too many watches" phenomenon as the underlying cause of the confusion and contention surrounding the often-conflicting answers to common business questions, such as these:

- How many customers do we have?
- How many products did we sell?
- How much revenue did we generate?

Therefore, another example of metadata is providing clear definitions of what the terms customers, products, and revenue actually mean.

The metadata associated with the data used to form the basis of the answers to these questions can cause a "framing effect," where the answer is correct from a certain point of view (that is, depending on which watch you're using to tell time). Therefore, you should always verify the metadata as well as the data.

It's okay to own more than one watch. After all, there's more than one time zone. So, when someone asks you what time it is, instead of responding in your local time (correct from your perspective), you should ask, "Where in the world are you?"

In the comments section of Henrik's blog post, I paraphrased King Claudius (from *Hamlet*):

The labels attached to critical data must not unwatched go.

THOUGHTS

- How do you define metadata?
- How do you use metadata in your organization?

- What's the relationship between metadata and data quality?
- Do you think metadata is (or should be considered) a dimension of data quality?

Idea 92: Completeness Is a Two-Way Street
Rich Murnane

One of the primary tenets of data quality programs is to ensure data is complete. Data quality practitioners (including me) typically determine completeness by reviewing the contents of database tables and fields and determining the number of records or fields that don't have values assigned to them when they probably should. We then ensure that if they do have values, the values make sense.

An example of such activity might be performed on a product database table for a large product distributor. To determine completeness, the product distributor's data management team would review the properties and business rules of its product database table to determine which fields need to have values and what those values should look like. The team will then likely perform some sort of data profiling exercise to determine how many records have null (or incorrect) values for these columns that they determined to be important. Once the team has completed the profiling exercise, it would probably come back and socialize that N percent of the records have missing/incorrect values. Hopefully the team will then store the output of this exercise, and it can perform the exercise again without too much effort.

> Completeness is a two-way street: breadth and depth.

Although the output of exercises like these is useful and we'd assume that it's important to know, we also need to consider the possibility that we might have missing records. How do we account for those?

I spend most of my time these days working on travel data, and I can tell you that completeness is most definitely a two-way street. Not only do we need to know that the records we have are complete, we need to know if we have all the records we should have. Obviously this is a challenge; how do you know what you don't know? When I need to discuss "completeness," I like to use the terms "breadth" and "depth." I explain that breadth resembles the review of the attributes of the records you have, and depth is trying to figure out what records you should have but perhaps don't have. Depending on your circumstances, determining the depth completeness of your data might be as easy as mining other database tables for records that should exist (for example, searching through sales order records for products that are not in your product table). On the other hand, you might need to perform some sort of audit on your data, which is what we typically do on the travel data management side. These audits are time consuming and not much fun, but they're necessary to ensure we have processes in place to account for all the data we should have.

Completeness is a two-way street: breadth and depth. Do you have a process in place to check for missing records? If so, I'd love to hear about it.

Idea 93: Technology and People Issues
Jim Harris

Extending the topic of my idea "predictably poor data quality" (see Idea 24) to include metadata, Beth Breidenbach wrote the excellent blog post "Predictably Poor MetaData Quality,"[viii] in which she explained how "similar human motivations come into play for metadata quality as with data quality."

> Only people can resolve people issues.

According to Breidenback,

> Human behavior is both the root cause and the solution. Technology doesn't cause or solve the data quality challenge. Rather, it's a tool that exacerbates or aids human behavior in either direction.

I agree. I've always found it puzzling when organizations try to resolve people issues by applying more technology or simply better technology. Only people can resolve people issues.

A big part of the problem is the fact that the word "data" is prevalent in the names we've given industry disciplines and enterprise information initiatives: data management, data architecture, data administration, data quality, data integration, data warehousing, and data governance—to name but a few.

Even the simplistic definition of metadata as "data about data" can make metadata management sound like a recursive reinforcement of the supremacy of data.

Idea 94: Data Transcendentalism
Jim Harris

In the comments of Idea 91, "What's the Meta with Your Data?"[ix] I coined the term "data transcendentalism," which is a reference to the 19th century philosophical movement started by, among others, Ralph Waldo Emerson, whom I now paraphrase:

> *So shall we come to look at the world of data with new eyes.*
>
> *We shall find answers to the endless inquiries of business insight. What is a shared version of the truth? What is the importance of high-quality data? What is the purpose of data governance?*
>
> *Only your people, and not data, business process, or technology, can answer these questions.*

> Although people, business process, data, and technology are all important, by far the most important of all is people.

> *Build, therefore, your own data management best practices.*
>
> *The faster you can avail your entire organization of the business understanding already present within your unique culture, but not yet shared across the enterprise, the sooner you will realize your organization's great potential.*
>
> *A corresponding reliance on the human side of business will transcend data, business process, and technology, and it will be your people who will lead the way.*

Although people, business process, data, and technology are all important, by far the most important of all is people.

Therefore, before you become too immersed in the intricate and low-level details of any of the many industry disciplines and enterprise information initiatives that start with data, I highly recommend that you consider data transcendentalism.

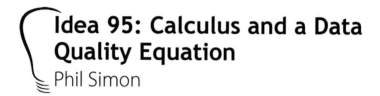

Idea 95: Calculus and a Data Quality Equation
Phil Simon

One of the benefits of cohosting *The Knights of the Data Roundtable*[5] is that I get to talk to some smart folks. Recently, Jim Harris and I had the pleasure of speaking with Peter Benson of the Electronic Commerce Code Management Association.

(Warning: I'm going to throw some calculus at you here. You have been forewarned.)

During the course of our conversation, Benson mentioned that data quality was exclusively a function of data requirements. That is, good requirements mean good data quality. Case closed.

To paraphrase Benson, you can't have good data quality without good data requirements. The latter was a necessary condition of the former. I honestly had never thought of data quality in that context before. I thought quite a bit about that comment for several days. Something just didn't sit right with me.

> Is data quality a function of good requirements and good metadata?

A few days later during our weekly tweet jam, I posed the following question on Twitter: is data quality a function of good requirements and good metadata? Or, for you calculus geeks out there:

Data Quality = f(Good Requirements, Good Metadata)

AN EXAMPLE

Let's look at customers at Acme, Inc. Let's say that I have perfectly defined the following with respect to customer:

- The term itself—with the requisite buy-in from all parts of the business

---

5. This is a show hosted by Jim Harris and me in which we discuss data management issues with industry experts and practitioners—and have way too much fun in the process.

- The meaning of the term (from both business and technical standpoints)
- The relationships between customers and other important elements, such as products, orders, and the like

Now, let's say that everyone inside Acme is on the same page. No one disputes the meaning of customer anywhere in the organization—a state that I have never seen in my years of consulting. Even parties external to Acme, such as vendors and suppliers, are in complete agreement over what we mean by customers. Because of our pristine requirements and metadata, do we have perfect or near-perfect data quality?

SIMON SAYS

I'm honestly not sure about the answer to that last question. Is there a third variable, such as the human element? Does this simple calculation ignore that? Or is the human element already accounted for? By properly defining our requirements and metadata, have we already checked that box?

Idea 96: Good Data Is the New Black
Jill Dyché

Fashion is fickle, and today's fabulous frock can quickly become tomorrow's housecoat. I once owned a pair of gauchos. For you readers born after 1970, gauchos are a short version of bell-bottoms, or a long version of culottes, or—never mind. Suffice it to say that on a good day I could look positively de rigueur. And there was that Indian-themed poncho, circa 1975, complete with fringe. At the time I was mainstream chic. But if I wore it today in a public square I'd be stoned to death.

Colors, patterns, and fabrics may come and go, but black, as they say, is always in style. Packing my carry-on for a recent trip to New York was super easy. Casually fling a pencil skirt, a few pairs of tights, a turtleneck, patent leather pumps, and some pearls—all of them black—into the garment bag (yes, also black), and you're ready for a couple days' worth of client meetings, a play, and dinner at Balthazar!

(Truth be told it rained in torrents, and I stuck to my hotel room where I had room service in my lime green Life Is Good flannel PJs, but I like the image of flinging a totally black wardrobe into my luggage in an Audrey-Hepburn-meets-Betty-Hutton kind of way, so please don't rain on my parade.)

This brings me to data quality. I think good data is the new black. After all, it makes everything so much more straight-forward. With good data, marketing campaigns are more relevant. Risk scoring is more accurate. Reporting to the street or to the feds is more reliable. You can take good data to a service-oriented architecture and make the whole thing so much better. You can take it to a call center rep and boost your customer satisfaction scores. You can take good data out like a debutante, waltz it around your company, and brag about what a promising future it has!

> Good, clean, standardized, reconciled, matched, integrated data is a business basic, and until we embrace the formal mechanisms to clean it up, we're simply mixing plaids with stripes.

Not having good data is way more risky. We skip development steps, demur in investing in automation, and ignore data correction prior to application deployment. Everyone knows it's a crapshoot, but people still try to pull it off. Bad data is the fashion version of wearing yellow: very few can really get away with it. And for those who try and fail, the consequences can be disastrous.

Sartorial metaphors aside, we've reached an era requiring good, clean, integrated data. It's the time for investing in automation. Convince your management that enterprise data management is no longer an intellectual pursuit; it's a bona fide need. It's time to take data quality out of the project and into the enterprise. Good, clean, standardized, reconciled, matched, integrated data is a business basic, and until we embrace the formal mechanisms to clean it up, we're simply mixing plaids with stripes.

Idea 97: Physical Data Models
Joyce Norris-Montanari

I've written before about subject area models (SAs or SAMs) and logical data models (LDMs). The next step, in our modeling adventure, is the physical data model (PDM). The PDM takes the required portions of the

LDM toward a technical solution, based on the platform. A platform is the hardware and software designated for the business and technical solution. Again, the PDM for our MDM solution of customer and product would only hold information about those sub-ject areas needed for the business and technical solution.

> A product is made up of multiple parts, but we may "physically" model all this infor-mation into one table.

Although the PDM looks like the LDM, it may not have all the detail. For example, in the PDM, we may take two logical tables and denormalize them into one table. A good example could be a product hierarchy. A product is made up of multiple parts, but we may "physi-cally" model all this information into one table. This would make querying the information easier on the reporting/analytic tools. That said, the rule must say that product, and its perspective parts, are always queried together. So we denormalize for a reason—which is usually performance in read or query, or efficiency in update or load.

Based on our physical technology or solution, the PDM may take the shape of a fact table for a data mart, which is queried quickly by our report-ing and analytic tools. All the business rules, the data models, are created and used in a business solution.

Idea 98: How to Succeed in Business
Jill Dyché

(In which Jill rips off a movie title to share a few observations.)

I'm not a sociologist or a socio-anthropologist. I'm also not a forensic psychologist or even an apologist. I have no Ph.D. in organizational dy-namics. I was a liberal arts major, and my graduate studies were in French. (*Tant pis.*) Although not credentialed in behavioral studies, I'm neverthe-less an avid observer of people, and it so happens that IT consulting is the perfect job if you're a student of human nature. As a fellow student, you've probably discovered that there is no lecture for this class. There's no text-book. No, you can't get a soft copy of the handouts.

I've learned many truisms about behavior in business in my years, and I thought I'd share a handful of them here:

- **Stop with all the meetings:** There are too many meetings because there's not enough ownership. You don't have to memorize *Death by Meeting* to understand that the need for consensus is inversely proportional to the existence of decision rights. And why don't decision rights exist at most companies? Because then people would be on the hook to actually deliver something. They'd be measured on their performance. And we can't have that now, can we?

  [Okay. That was a little too cynical. Maybe a bit too freshly minted. I'll lighten up on the next one.]

- **Show your management Number 1:** Management doesn't know it. Managers are too busy managing by personality and not looking at the work.

  [That wasn't very diplomatic. Don't worry; the next one's a softball.]

- **Stop caring too much:** It compromises your credibility. The phrase, "OmiGOD, there's a dangling foreign key in that logical model; we need to have a meeting *right now!*" should not leave your lips. Variations on this theme include writing emails in capital letters, making public examples of people's foibles (professionally and otherwise), and "getting everyone in a room." More subtly, people who care too much often emit guttural noises from the larynx like, "Humph!" or "Grrrrr!" when they're vexed. If you have a Big Idea and no one's listening,

  > Circle back with introverts after meetings and get their thoughts.

  they're not ready for the message yet. So wait. You can always finger-wag and say, "I told you so" later.

- **Never finger-wag and say "I told you so":** There are many reasons not to do this, and you heard them all from your mom, so I won't list them here. This morning I took a call from a VP who'd issued a request for proposal (RFP) last year and didn't choose my firm. "We should have used you guys," he admitted sheepishly. "We were stupidly price-sensitive, and it's been eight months and I've got nothing."

Humph! Grrrrr!

[See what I just did there? Don't do that.]

"How do we engage you guys?" he said.

"We can be there next week," I said.

- **Honor the introverts:** You have colleagues who like to hang in the doorways of people's cubicles and chat. They think out loud and have a lot of meetings. These are the extroverts. They get their energy from human interaction and like immediate feedback.

  You also have colleagues who don't pipe up in meetings. They're the introverts. They're thinking in their heads where, I'd argue, the thinking *should* be done. They're processing what's been discussed (usually by the extroverts). That music you hear at the end of every staff meeting? It's the introverts quietly singing, "Free at last, thank God Almighty, I'm free at last!" Circle back with introverts after meetings and get their thoughts. Solicit their ideas in writing. Just because they're not vocal doesn't mean they're not savvy and full of Big Ideas.

- **Quit the chest beating:** They knew from your email signature and your voicemail greeting—and, admit it, from the lipstick on the restroom mirror—that your employer is the biggest [x] in the [y] industry, or that your company was the first-to-market with the i-whatever, or that your boss's boss's boss was mentioned in a sidebar on Forbes.com. You might even be a decision maker at this Big Company. Remember this: if it doesn't matter in five years, it doesn't matter. (Strike me down if that's not a direct quote from none other than Cher.)

Idea 99: Being Horizontally Vertical

Jim Harris

Most organizations are naturally vertically aligned, meaning that they're organized by functional area, line of business, or some other division of labor. These vertical silos allow the organization to focus specialists on specific business areas.

As a general example, accountants usually work in Finance, database administrators work in IT, marketers work in Marketing, and salespeople work in Sales. And as an insurance industry line of business example, specialists in car insurance work in Auto, specialists in health insurance work in Health, and specialists in life insurance work in Life.

> This vertical orientation creates organizational silos that lose sight of the fact that the sum of silos is one horizontal enterprise.

Of course, this division of labor makes sense because most of the daily operations of the organization must be carried out by people who have been trained in a specific type of business activity.

However, when taken to its extremes, this vertical orientation creates organizational silos that lose sight of the fact that the sum of silos is one horizontal enterprise. According to enterprise mathematics, in an organization with five functional silos, $1 + 1 + 1 + 1 + 1 = 1$ (not 5).

Just as we can't see the forest through the trees, we can't see the enterprise through the silos.

This state of affairs presents a complex challenge for enterprise-wide initiatives, such as data quality, master data management, and data governance, which require a cross-functional alignment. In this alignment, the group identities of vertical silos reidentify with the super-group identity of the horizontal enterprise.

These initiatives try to encourage horizontal collaboration across the organization's vertical silos, which requires some vertical sacrifices for the horizontal greater good. This involves striking a balance between allowing verticals to continue their unique contributions to the enterprise's success and requiring that they also dedicate some of their resources (money, time, people) to horizontal efforts, which, in the short term, may be somewhat disruptive to their vertical efforts.

In other words, the enterprise-wide initiatives require the organizational silos to find ways to be horizontally vertical.

Have you found ways to be horizontally vertical?

Idea 100: Name Patterns and Parsing
David Loshin

I'm sometimes astounded by the variety in which Anglicized names can appear in content. A few years back I was working on a small utility that parsed American names, and I was lucky enough to review a list of name string patterns used by folks at the U.S. Census Bureau. You'd be surprised at the number of variant formats, even just relying on five token types:

- Title
- First Name
- Initial
- Last Name
- Suffix (generational or subtitle, such as "ESQ")

Add in some punctuation (such as periods, commas, ampersands), and the result is hundreds of variations. Once you allow for two entities to share a name string ("Mr. and Mrs. John Smith"), you end up with a lot more, because there are variations on that format as well.

To be able to recognize a name pattern, an algorithm must be able to identify the tokens (such as first name or last name) and then determine if the token sequence shows up as a pattern in the pattern set. This would be challenging enough, but here are a few more:

> To be able to recognize a name pattern, an algorithm must be able to identify the tokens (such as first name or last name) and then determine if the token sequence shows up as a pattern in the pattern set.

- This works moderately well as long as each token is uniquely distinctive. It becomes more challenging when a name chunk can resolve to more than one token. For example, "Jackson" is both a last name and a first name.
- There needs to be a comprehensive set of reference tables that describe the sets of values for each of the token types.
- This starts to not work so well when there are errors in the token strings, unless there are ways to interpolate the correct

string. When the strings are not mapped to tokens, there will be no matching patterns.

So although the concept is straightforward, there are some twists to keep the process interesting.

Idea 101: Data, Priorities, and Muhammad Ali
Phil Simon

In preparing for my panel discussion at the DataFlux IDEAS Conference, I decided that I wasn't going to be doing an extensive amount of preparation. At least in the business and technology worlds, I like to think that I know what I'm talking about. Plus, I enjoy fresh presentations and tend to shy away from overly polished ones.

However, I've been thinking a good bit about a quote from Muhammad Ali: "Don't count the days; make the days count." Although he surely wasn't talking about data quality, governance, or management, it's apropos for the panel—and for everyday life in the world of information management, really.

CHOOSING YOUR BATTLES

With respect to data, no organization is completely governed or completely undisciplined. These states represent different ends of the same continuum. To be sure, some organizations manage their data much better than others, but even the former have their challenges. What separates the good from the bad and the ugly?

Well, I could write a book about that topic, and perhaps one day I will. For one, let's focus on the ability of progressive organizations to successfully choose their battles. Perhaps driven by dynamic leaders and buoyed by pragmatic cultures, some companies simply do a better job of the following:

- At a high level, recognizing the importance of data—and good data
- Employing the right resources (read: software, external, internal) to get the job done

- Proactively addressing would-be issues
- Getting out in front of actual issues
- Resolving the biggest issues first
- Circling back to pesky minor issues before they become much larger ones

> Data quality is a mind-set, not a series of standalone initiatives.

- Praising those who discover issues—not excoriating them
- Removing those who show a consistent disregard to data quality and integrity
- Recognizing that data quality is a mind-set, not a series of standalone initiatives

SIMON SAYS

Ours is not a perfect world. If given infinite time, resources, and money, many organizations would find themselves in vastly superior places compared to today. Alas, we have to make trade-offs and sacrifices. The question is: what are they?

Although the results vary based on myriad factors such as industry, organizational age, size, and the like, organizations that make the best trade-offs tend to be more successful. They get the most bang for their buck. In other words, these organizations make their days count.

Some projects and initiatives are poorly conceived from the start. Smart companies get away from them as soon as possible, recognizing that sunk costs cannot be recovered.

Further Readings and Resources

BOOKS

Cervo, Dalton and Mark Allen. *Master Data Management in Practice: Achieving True Customer MDM.*

Dyché, Jill and Evan Levy. *Customer Data Integration.*

Fisher, Tony. *The Data Asset: How Smart Companies Govern Their Data for Business Success.*

Loshin, David. *The Practitioner's Guide to Data Quality Improvement.*

Loshin, David. *Master Data Management.*

Simon, Phil. *The Next Wave of Technologies: Opportunities in Chaos.*

Simon, Phil. *Why New Systems Fail: An Insider's Guide to Successful IT Projects.*

THE DATAFLUX KNOWLEDGE CENTER
Read customer case studies, industry reports, and white papers from leading data management experts:
www.dataflux.com/Resources/DataFlux-Resources.aspx

Ideas by Contributor

The following text lists each idea and page number by contributor.

Dylan Jones

David Loshin

Glossary

BOB: A best of breed (BOB) approach to enterprise systems involves purchasing applications from different vendors and stitching them together. For example, a company may purchase a human resources package from one vendor and an accounting package from another.

business process: The defined method for a range of activities that organizations perform daily. A business can include anything from the steps needed to make a product to the way a supply is ordered or how an invoice is created. Excellent data quality and governance allow organizations to automate some business processes.

business rules: The defined operations and constraints that help organizations conduct activities in efficient, profit-making, and legal ways. An example of a business rule for a hospital would be that no male patient can be marked pregnant. Organizations typically have thousands of business rules, but not all facets of the same organizations follow all of them—and, in some cases, the rules can conflict.

canned reports: Vendors ship their applications with many canned or standard reports that present data in a predefined way.

custom reports: User-created reports that present data in a way required by the client; vendors do not ship their products with custom reports.

dashboard: Like the part in a car it's named after, a business dashboard allows executives to see key metrics about anything from monthly sales to manufacturing downtime sent via email or available on an internal website.

data attributes: A characteristic of a block of data, such as whether it comes in numbers (phone numbers, zip codes) or words (street name, last name).

data cleansing: The process of reviewing data to make sure it's correct, up-to-date, and not duplicated.

data governance: The process for addressing how data enters the organization, who is accountable for it, and how—using people, processes, and technologies—data achieves a quality standard that allows for complete transparency within an organization.

data profiling: A process for looking at the data within the source systems and understanding the data elements and the anomalies. A thorough data profiling exercise alerts organizations to data that does not meet the characteristics defined in the metadata compiled during data exploration. Data profiling can also tell organizations if the data meets business needs and determine relationships across data sources.

data steward: Critical players in data governance councils. Comfortable with technology and business problems, data stewards seek to speak up for their business units when an organization-wide decision won't work for that business unit. They are not turf protectors; instead, they seek solutions that will work across an organization.

database trigger: A database trigger defines an action the database should take when some database-related event occurs. For example, an AP clerk pays a vendor's invoice, an action that triggers an automatic email to the head of accounts payable.

database view: Database views take data from multiple tables and present them in a single database object, making reporting simpler than if the tables remained separate.

enterprise resource planning system: *See* ERP system.

ERP system: An enterprise resource planning (ERP) system stitches together an organization's back office operations. Specifically, these systems create and store data related to the following types of transactions: manufacturing, supply chain management, finance and accounting, HR, and customer relationship management (CRM). Of course, this depends on what individual organizations choose to utilize.

executive sponsor: A C-level executive engaged in data governance and the process of achieving that goal.

hybrids: End users who understand the front end of an application as well as the corresponding "back end" of tables, data structures, and fields. Hybrids are often able to solve functional and technical problems with equal aplomb.

identity resolution: Is John Q. Smith the same as John Quincy Smith? Using address and other data identity resolution techniques, companies can purge their files of multiple versions of the same customer or the same product listed under multiple names. Identify resolution does go beyond matching in that it looks at a series of attributes (phone number, identifying number) to test for similarities.

index: A table index is essentially a way of uniquely identifying each record on a table. Indexing offers significant benefits. First, indexes increase database performance. Second, databases enforce referential integrity. A typical index might be an employee number. That way, an organization can employ 100 people named Bruce Springsteen, but each would have his own unique identifier, which is a good thing.

interface: An interface takes data from one system to be imported, exported, or updated by another system. On new system projects, interfaces from carriers or vendors typically have to be rewritten to reference the new system.

JOIN: SQL JOIN statements essentially allow end users to retrieve data from multiple tables. There are numerous types of JOINs for many purposes. Many complex reports and queries (and often some simple ones) require joins to pull data from different tables.

legacy system: "A system needs to be considered in terms of its ability to support the current and future processes of an organization; an inability to support changing process requirements is now taken as the definition of a legacy system." This definition of the term comes from *An Executive's Guide to Information Technology: Principles, Business Models, and Terminology.* In the book, Robert Plant and Stephen Murrell explain, at a high level, the decision to purchase and implement a new system.

master data: Also known as reference data, this data describes the important details of a business subject. Master data gives an accurate, 360-degree view of the business subject.

master data management (MDM): The guiding principles for maintaining master data in a manner that can be shared across various systems and departments throughout an organization.

MDM: *See* master data management.

metadata: The data about the organization's data, found in every data source throughout the enterprise. Metadata describes the information in these data resources.

parallel test: In a parallel test, identical data is loaded or entered into two disparate systems for testing purposes. The results are then compared. In theory, the output should be similar, if not identical. Legitimate system differences often persist, however, because no two systems are exactly the same.

Sarbanes-Oxley Act: *See* SOX.

scope creep: Scope creep takes place when the project initially sets out to accomplish X. However, based on a number of factors, the project now must accomplish X, Y, and Z. For projects sold as fixed bids, the system integrator (SI) avoids scope creep.

shelfware: A moniker for software that organizations have purchased but not implemented/activated.

SI:	*See* system integrator.

SOX: In 2002, President Bush signed into law the Sarbanes-Oxley Act (SOX) in response to a number of highly publicized accounting scandals involving large U.S. companies. The bill was designed to increase corporate responsibility and auditing requirements. SOX was named after sponsors Senator Paul Sarbanes (D-Md.) and Representative Michael G. Oxley (R-Ohio).

SQL: Structured Query Language is a simple but powerful programming language that allows selecting, updating, adding, and deleting of data from tables.

spend management: The method that organizations use to control and optimize the money they spend. It seeks to achieve one view of all spending from sourcing supplies to settling bills and then looks for ways to cut spending or consolidate purchases to achieve greater savings.

Structured Query Language: *See* SQL.

supply chain management: The management of business units in the provision of products and services. It spans the movement and storage of raw materials, work-in-process inventory, and finished goods from point-of-origin to point-of-consumption.

system design: Phase of system implementations in which end users configure the system to meet the organization's business needs.

system integrators (SIs): Consulting firms that specialize in migrating their clients from one system to another.

About the Contributors

Jill Dyché

Jill's role at DataFlux is a combination of best-practice expert, key client advisor, and all-around thought leader. She is responsible for industry education, key client strategies, and market analysis in the areas of data governance, business intelligence, master data management, and customer relationship management. Jill is a regularly featured speaker and the author of several books. Jill's latest book, *Customer Data Integration: Reaching a Single Version of the Truth* (Wiley & Sons, 2006), was coauthored with Evan Levy and shows the business breakthroughs achieved with integrated customer data. She believes that Def Leppard, mixed-breed dogs, and Oprah's *O* magazine are terribly underrated. She is certain that no one has made an edible cabbage roll since her mother died. You can follow her at @jilldyche.

Dylan Jones

Dylan Jones is the founder of Data Quality Pro and Data Migration Pro, popular online communities that provide a range of practical resources and support to their respective professions. Dylan has an extensive information management background and is a prolific publisher of expert articles and tutorials on all manner of data-related initiatives.

David Loshin

David Loshin, president of Knowledge Integrity, Inc., is a recognized thought leader and expert consultant in the areas of data quality, master data management, and business intelligence. David is a prolific author regarding data management best practices, via the expert channel at b-eye-network.com and numerous books, white papers, and web seminars on a variety of data management best practices. His book *Business Intelligence: The Savvy Manager's Guide* (June 2003) has been hailed as a resource allowing readers to "gain an understanding of business intelligence, business management disciplines, data warehousing, and how all of the pieces work together." His book *Master Data Management* has been endorsed by data management industry leaders, and his valuable MDM insights can be reviewed at mdmbook.com. David is also the author of the upcoming book *The Practitioner's Guide to Data Quality Improvement*. He can be reached at loshin@knowledge-integrity.com.

Jim Harris

Jim Harris is the blogger-in-chief at Obsessive-Compulsive Data Quality (*www.ocdqblog.com*), an independent blog offering a vendor-neutral perspective on data quality and its related disciplines. Jim is a recognized industry thought leader on data quality with more than 15 years of professional services and application development experience in data quality, data integration, data warehousing, business intelligence, master data management, and data governance. He is also an independent consultant, speaker, and freelance writer. Jim is active on Twitter, where you can follow him at @ocdqblog.

Rich Murnane

Richard Murnane is a data architect and enterprise data operations manager. As leader of the iJET Enterprise Data Operations team, Rich and his team are responsible for the collection, processing, monitoring, and quality of client and iJET production data. Rich has 14 years of experience designing, building, and supporting database systems. He is an active member of the Data Administrator Management Association (DAMA) (National Capitol Region Chapter) and Mid-Atlantic Oracle User Group. He is a founding member of the iJET Professional Services team, which provides travel industry and data management services for corporate and federal government clients. As an active member of the data management community, Rich has been blogging about data management for more than five years. He is also a member of the DataFlux Client Advisory Board. He holds a Bachelor of Science from Salisbury University with concentrations in computer science and mathematics.

Joyce Norris-Montanari

Joyce Norris-Montanari, CBIP-CDMP, is president of DBTech Solutions, Inc. Joyce advises clients on all aspects of architectural integration, business intelligence, and data management. She advises clients about technology, including tools such as ETL, profiling, database, quality, and metadata. Joyce speaks frequently at data warehouse conferences and is a contributor to several trade publications. She coauthored *Data Warehousing and E-Business* (John Wiley & Sons) with William H. Inmon and others. Joyce has managed and implemented data integrations, data warehouses, and operational data stores in industries including education, pharmaceutical, restaurants, telecommunications, government, health care, financial, oil and gas, insurance, research and development, and retail.

Phil Simon

Phil Simon is the author of *The New Small* (Motion, 2010), *Why New Systems Fail* (Cengage, 2010), *The Next Wave of Technologies* (John Wiley & Sons, 2010), and *The Age of the Platform* (Motion, 2011). A recognized technology expert, he consults companies on how to optimize their use of technology. His contributions have been featured on ZDNet, Technorati, the American Express Open Forum, *ComputerWorld*, *The New York Times*, *The Globe and Mail*, ReadWriteWeb, abcnews.com, forbes.com, and many other sites.

His main website is *www.philsimonsystems.com*, and his Twitter handle is @philsimon.

About DataFlux

DataFlux enables business agility and IT efficiency by providing innovative data management technology and services that transform data into a strategic asset, helping you reduce costs, optimize revenue, and mitigate risks. A wholly owned subsidiary of SAS, DataFlux helps organizations manage critical aspects of data through unified technologies and expertise that provide the benefits of data quality, data integration, and master data management.

DataFlux offers complete enterprise solutions, including:

- Enterprise data quality
- Data integration, migration, and consolidation
- Master data management (MDM)
- Data governance

Founded in 1997, DataFlux has evolved from a provider of data cleansing tools to an international market-leading provider of enterprise data quality, data integration, and master data management solutions. DataFlux helps customers rapidly assess and improve problematic data, delivering the high-quality information that fuels successful enterprise efforts that reduce costs, increase operational efficiency, and enable governance, risk, and compliance management.

DataFlux is headquartered in Cary, North Carolina, with international headquarters in London and offices in France, Germany, and Australia. For more information, please see *www.dataflux.com*.

About the Editor

Phil Simon is the author of *The New Small* (Motion, 2010), *Why New Systems Fail* (Cengage, 2010), *The Next Wave of Technologies* (John Wiley & Sons, 2010), and *The Age of the Platform* (Motion, 2011). A recognized technology expert, he consults companies on how to optimize their use of technology. His contributions have been featured on ZDNet, Technorati, the American Express Open Forum, *ComputerWorld*, *The New York Times*, *The Globe and Mail*, ReadWriteWeb, abcnews.com, forbes.com, and many other sites.

His main website is *www.philsimonsystems.com*, and his Twitter handle is @philsimon.

Endnotes

i. www.jilldyche.com/2010/04/the-tyranny-of-consensus.html

ii. www.youtube.com/watch?v=5XD2kNopsUs&feature= player_embedded

iii. http://dpadvantage.wordpress.com/2009/11/12/there-is- no-such-thing-as-a-data-quality-problem/

iv. www.dataqualitypro.com/data-quality-home/iqm-cmm- information-quality-management-capability-maturity-m.html

v. http://sheezaredhead.wordpress.com/

vi. http://www.information-management.com/ issues/21_2/MDM_data_management_quality_BI_ governance-10019873-1.html

vii. http://liliendahl.wordpress.com/2010/01/09/ perfect-wrong-answer/

viii. http://datageekgal.blogspot.com/2010/06/predictably-poor- metadata-quality.html

ix. www.dataroundtable.com/?p=1624

Index

VPN (virtual private network), security too
    cumbersome, 30–31

W–Z
Wanless, Jill, 106
working hard, effort delusion, 51

you touch it, you buy it approach, 83–84

CPSIA information can be obtained at www.ICGtesting.com
Printed in the USA
BVOW041502050312

284456BV00001B/14/P